HELPING MEN

A PSYCHOANALYTIC APPROACH

LORETTA R. LOEB, MD

and

FELIX F. LOEB, JR., MD

IPBOOKS.net
International Psychoanalytic Books

A Division of International Psychoanalytic Media Group

Distributed by Jason Aronson, Inc.

Published by International Psychoanalytic Books (IPBooks)
25–79 31st Street; Astoria, NY 11102
www.IPBooks.net

Distributed by Jason Aronson, Inc.

ISBN: 978-0-9851329-2-7

Library of Congress Control Number: 2012945249

CONTENTS

ACKNOWLEDGMENTS

For their support

Charles W. Socarides, MD
Dr. Socarides supported and encouraged our work.
So did the members of his Discussion Group at
the American Psychoanalytic Association.

Sylvia Brody, PhD

Martin Richardson, MD

Felix F. Loeb, Jr., M.D. and Loretta R. Loeb M.D.

INTRODUCTION AND OVERVIEW

We do not specialize in, nor seek, patients with sexually deviant behavior. Occasionally, however, such patients have sought and received psychoanalytic treatment from us. Like Freud's fetishistic patients, our patients sought treatment for their painful neurotic symptoms, not for their pleasurable sexually deviant behaviors.

In this book, we summarize the psychoanalytic treatments of seven male patients who engaged in homosexual, fetishistic, transvestite, or gender identity behaviors (Freud 1927). As children, each of these patients had observed that females lacked penises and had inferred that they were castrated males. This caused them to fear that they too could become castrated. In some of our patients this fear was intensified when they construed that a caretaker was actually threatening them with castration. The psychoanalysis of these patients' dreams, symptoms, and transference reactions, revealed that in childhood each of them had experienced a conflict between his fear of the loss of his penis and his fear of the loss of his maternal object. Because, as children, they were unable to resolve this conflict, they each had repressed this conflict into their unconscious minds. Thus, they each had developed an unconscious conflict between their castration-anxiety and their separation-anxiety. Each of them had dealt with this unconscious conflict by identifying with their psychologically castrating maternal object and by changing the aim and/or the object of their sexual drive.

In his transference reactions to his psychoanalyst, each of our patients attempted to replicate the situations that led to the unconscious conflicts that led to his aberrant sexual behavior. Once these transference reactions were interpreted to, and understood by, our patients, they became consciously aware of their formerly repressed heterosexual inclinations.

In Chapter 1, we review Freud's and his followers' writings about sexual deviations. In Chapters 2 and 3 we describe our psychoanalytic treatments of two homosexual men. The psychoanalysis of a man with a foot fetish is presented in Chapter 4; Chapters 5 and 6 summarize the successful psychoanalytic treatments of two men who suffered from transvestite symptoms. The treatments of two boys with gender-identity problems are presented in Chapter 7. In Chapter 8, we show that the two genetically unrelated patients described in Chapters 6 and 7 developed their similar sexual disturbances because of virtually identical environmental determinants.

We treated each of these patients using the psychoanalytic clinical research method. That is, we did not impose any theoretically preconceived expectations—derived from the psychoanalytic literature—onto them. The use of this research method was extremely important in making the treatment of each of these patients successful.

We followed up with most of these patients and found that they remained free of their sexual deviations for many years. Psychotherapists should not believe that all sexual deviations are not changeable through psychotherapy because they are genetically determined.

REFERENCE

FREUD, S. (1927). Fetishism. *Standard Edition* 21:152–153.

LITERATURE REVIEW OF THE PSYCHOANALYTIC UNDERSTANDING OF NORMAL AND DEVIANT SEXUAL DEVELOPMENT

In this chapter we first review Freud's clinical observations and theoretical conclusions about sexual perversions. What Freud and Fenichel called "sexual perversions" we now call "sexual deviations." Since we find no mention of transvestitism in Freud's writings, we then review Otto Fenichel's writings about this condition. We then review subsequent authors' clinical observations and theoretical conclusions about sexual perversions.

In 1896, Freud wrote to his friend Flies that it was wrong to suppose that sexual life only begins during puberty. Then, in 1905, in his book *Three Essays on the Theory of Sexuality* (p.172), Freud again asserted that sexuality is present in childhood. At the time most people disputed Freud's claim and believed that sexuality began in puberty as a powerful attraction exercised by one sex upon the other with the *aim* of pleasurable genital sexual union. These people failed to understand that Freud had expanded his definition of the word "sexuality" to include the oral and anal pleasurable *aims* that are present in childhood and, subsequently, in puberty, become part of preparatory sexual foreplay. Today, most people realize that both pregenital and genital sexuality occur in children. Freud stated that most people have "infantile amnesia" and forget the beginnings of their own sexual lives. He discovered that children's early sexual experiences could lead them to have either normal sexual lives, neuroses, or perversions.

Freud (1916, p. 305) observed that most people have perverse inclinations, which have roots in childhood, in a latent form. These latent inclinations can subsequently be brought out by deprivation of normal sexual outlets. Freud said that perverse sexuality is nothing other than infantile sexuality, magnified and split up into its separate impulses.

In his *Three Essays,* Freud called the person toward whom a sexual attraction is directed, the *sexual object,* and the sexual act which is directed toward this person the *sexual aim.* He observed that sexual deviations could occur both in a person's choice of a sexual object and a person's choice of a sexual aim. Freud said that every external or internal factor that hinders or postpones the attainment of the normal sexual aim of sexual union would eventually lend support to a tendency to linger over the preparatory activities (the foreplay) and develop them into deviant sexual aims and/or objects.

FREUD'S VIEW OF THE
PSYCHODYNAMICS OF HOMOSEXUALITY

In his *Three Essays,* Freud rejected the current medical explanation for homosexuality: that it was an innate indication of nervous degeneracy. He argued that homosexuality occurred in too many otherwise normal and, even, gifted and highly-developed persons to be regarded as a sign of some kind of organic (genetic) degeneration. Freud said that homosexuality could not be fully explained either by the hypothesis that it was genetically determined or by the hypothesis that it was acquired through experience. He did not believe that homosexuality could be traced to certain localized centers of the brain because evolutionary evidence in normal adult anatomy pointed toward "an originally bisexual physical disposition" in everyone. Freud (1905) believed that in addition to a narcissistic object choice and a fear of castration, the retention of the erotic significance of the anal zone was of great importance as a determinant of homosexuality. He said (Freud 1916) that people with sexual perversions [deviations] behave toward their sexual objects in approximately the same way as normal people do to theirs. But that their sexual activity diverges widely from what seems desirable to most people. Freud said that the claim made by homosexuals that their homoerotic impulses are exceptions collapses when we learn that such impulses have been invariably discovered in every single neurotic, and that a fair number of their neurotic symptoms give expression to this latent homosexuality. Freud added that consciously and *manifestly* homosexual individuals are few compared to the number of *latently* homosexual individuals.

Freud (1916, p. 322) said, "The essence of the perversions lies not in the extension of the sexual aim, not in the replacement of the genitals, not even always in the variant choice of the object, but solely in the exclusiveness with which these deviations are carried out and as a result of which the sexual act serving the purpose of reproduction is put on one side. In so far as the perverse actions are inserted in the performance of the normal sexual act as preparatory or intensifying contributions, they are in reality not perversions at all [but foreplay]." Thus, in perversions the reproductive function is abandoned.

Freud (1905, pp. 153–154) divided sexually deviant persons into those who, like homosexuals, change their sexual *object* (that is, either a person or part of a person) and those who change their sexual *aim* (that is, their sexual act). The first group included those who renounce the union of the two genitals and who replace the genitals by some other part or region of the body. For example, they replace the vagina with the mouth or the anus. In choosing the anus, they disregard any feelings of disgust and select it because of its proximity to the vagina.

Freud (1920, pp. 150–151) recognized that it was difficult to cure homosexuality through psychoanalysis because one does not easily give up a sexual object that provides so much pleasure. He said that making a homosexual heterosexual was as difficult as making a heterosexual homosexual. Freud felt that in the majority of homosexuals it was not possible to develop "the blighted germs of heterosexual tendencies which are present in every homosexual" (1920, pp.145–172).

FREUD'S OBSERVATIONS AND
CONCLUSIONS ABOUT FETISHISTIC BEHAVIOR

In his *Three Essays* Freud said that fetishists abandon the genital as a sexual object and take some other part of the body as the object they desire—a woman's breast, foot, shoe, piece of hair, clothing, or under-clothing. Freud pointed out that a certain degree of fetishism is present in normal love, when the normal sexual object is, or seems to be, unattain-able. The situation only becomes pathological when the longing for the fetish passes beyond the point of being merely a necessary substitute for the normal sexual object and actually replaces it, becoming the *sole* sexual object. In 1938, Freud (pp. 202–203) said that fetishism is based on a patient (who is almost always male) not recognizing the fact that females have no penis. This fact is extremely undesirable to him since it proves that he too could be castrated. He therefore disavows his own sense-perception which showed him that females lack penises and holds fast to the conviction that they have penises. The disavowed perception does not, however, remain entirely without influence, for, in spite of everything, he has not had the courage to assert that he actually saw a penis. He takes hold of something else instead—some part of the body or some other object–and assigns to it the role of the penis which he cannot do without. It is usually something that he in fact saw at the moment at which he saw the female genitals. In other words, it is something that can suitably serve as a symbolic substitute for the penis. Freud said that the fetish is constructed as a compromise formed with the help of displacement, such as occurs in dreams. Thus, the fetish was created to destroy the evidence of the possibility of castration, so that the fear of castration could be avoided. Freud noted that some fetishists also still retain their fear of castration. Their behavior is therefore simultaneously expressing two contrary premises. On the one hand, they are disavowing the fact of their perception—the fact that they saw no penis in the female genital area. On the other hand, they are recognizing the fact that females have no penis and are drawing the correct conclusions from it. The two attitudes persist side by side throughout their lives without influencing each other. Freud said that this can be called a splitting of the ego and that in fetishists, therefore, the detachment of the ego from the reality of the external world has never succeeded completely. Freud went on to say that all fetishists retain an aversion to real female genitals and that this is a conscious indication that a repression has taken place (Freud 1927, p. 154).

FENICHEL'S VIEWS ON THE
PSYCHODYNAMICS OF TRANSVESTITISM

Fenichel (1945, p. 344) said that whereas the homosexual man replaces his love for his mother by an identification with her, the fetishist refuses to acknowledge that his mother has no penis. The male transvestite assumes both the attitude of the homosexual and the fetishist simultaneously. He overcomes his castration anxiety by fantasying that she has a penis, and identifies himself with this phallic woman. Thus, the fundamental trend of transvestitism is the same as that found in homosexuality and in fetishism: the refutation of the idea that there is a danger of castration. Fenichel said that the transvestite act has two unconscious meanings: (a) an object-erotic and fetishistic one: the person cohabits not with a woman but with her clothes, which symbolically represent her penis; (b) a narcissistic one: the transvestite himself represents the phallic woman under whose clothes a penis is hidden. Thus, the transvestite man proves to himself that the woman's penis is not lost.

Neither Freud nor Fenichel wrote about gender identity disorders.

VIEWS ON THE PSYCHODYNAMICS OF HOMOSEXUALITY AFTER FREUD

Anna Freud (1951, pp. 117–118; 1949) felt that to help a homosexual redirect his sexual interest toward a woman one must make him aware of his fear of being castrated by women, his fear of his own aggression, destructiveness, and sadism toward women and his fear of oral dependence on women. The active homosexual identifies with his passive partner, and the passive homosexual with the active partner. The passive homosexual, for example, first projects his own masculinity (his penis and secondary sexual characteristics) onto a partner and then recovers it by identifying with the partner and treasuring him as a possession. After this material is worked through and assimilated, the patient becomes potent heterosexually. Anna Freud felt that in order to achieve normality and the ability to love a woman, the fantasy of homosexuals that they would dissolve in the woman at the height of the sexual act must be analyzed and worked through.

George H. Wiedeman (1962, pp. 386–409) observed that there were few reports on transference, the course in therapy, and treatment results with homosexual patients. He (1974) surveyed the psychoanalytic literature between 1962 and 1972 and found eight works that significantly advanced the basic psychoanalytic understanding of psychosexual development, the formation of sexual identity, and the sexual deviations. A summary of these works follows.

Irving Bieber et al. (1962) studied 106 treated male homosexuals and matched them with 100 heterosexual controls. They found that "seventy-three per cent of the mothers of the homosexuals had extraordinarily preferential, intimate, seductive, inhibiting, and over controlling relations with their sons. In many instances their sons were more significant to them than were their husbands. These mothers usually discouraged their sons' masculine activities and attitudes, and encouraged their feminine ones. They allied themselves with their sons against the fathers, and established an intimate, confidante type of relationship with them, overprotected them from physical injury, and restricted their play, social, and other activities. Most of these mothers double-bound their sons by being sexually seductive to them while rejecting their masculine behaviors.

According to Bieber et al., 79 of the fathers of these homosexual sons were unusually detached and distant from their sons and did not furnish a model for masculine identification. Nor did they protect their sons from the above mentioned, destructive maternal influences. Some of the fathers reacted with hostility if their sons exhibited any masculine sexual behavior. Only three fathers were seductive toward their sons. When fathers of homosexual sons were not detached, the therapeutic results were more favorable. In comparison to other siblings the homosexual son was the least preferred by the father. The majority of homosexuals did not have homosexual siblings, yet the occurrence of homosexuality in the same family was higher than in the families of the non-homosexual control group. The 'classical' homosexual triangular pattern was one where the mother was dominant, close, binding, and intimate, with her son while being minimizing toward her husband, who was detached, and often hostile, toward his son.

The preadolescent behavior of the boys later to become homosexuals was significantly different from the behavior of the control group. They were excessively fearful of physical injury and avoided fights. Few homosexuals were athletic, participated in sports, or were well coordinated as children. Very few of the homosexuals played with boys as children, and a third of them played predominantly with girls. They were guilty over masturbation. They expressed a desire to be like women much more frequently than did the boys in the control group.

Twenty-nine of the 106 homosexuals who undertook treatment became exclusively heterosexual. The following factors improved the prognosis: (1) The patient was bisexual at the beginning of analysis. (2) The patient began analysis before age thirty-five. (3) The patient continued in analysis for at least 150 hours, preferably 350 hours or more. The longer the treatment, the better were the results. (4) The patient was motivated to become heterosexual. (5) The patient had a non-detached, or at least an ambivalent, father. (6) The patient's father liked women, respected and/or admired the patient, was affectionate, and was more intimate with the patient than with other male siblings. (7) The patient "idolized" women. (8) The patient had tried heterosexual genital contact at some time. (9) The patient had erotic heterosexual activity in the manifest content of his dreams.

Thus, Bieber et al.'s data confirmed and supplemented the psycho-analytic data regarding the environmental genesis of homosexuality that was presented by Freud and other analysts prior to this study. Its value lies in a description of various familial constellations that contribute to the development of homosexuality, and it presents further proof that homosexuality can be treated.

Socarides (1968), in his book, *The Overt Homosexual*, adds his own ideas on the genesis, psychodynamics, and the psychoanalytic treatment of homosexuals to the psychoanalytic literature. These ideas are based on clinical data from patients he had psychoanalyzed. Socarides found the use of analyzable parameters to be very helpful in psychoanalyzing homosexuals. He also recommended the judicious use of non-psychoanalytic measures—like those that Freud used with phobic patients. For example, Socarides would suggest to the homosexual patient that he seek out the phobically avoided woman. He pointed out that most descriptions of the psychoanalyses of homosexuals lacked a methodical presentation of the verbal and nonverbal communications between analyst and patient. Socarides felt that pregenital pathogenic factors originating in the undifferentiated symbiotic and individuation-separation phases of development were the most important determinants of homosexuality. For example, he describes patients who were severely threatened, by a regression to an early symbiotic stage, with a dissolution of their ego boundaries. Their wishes to penetrate the mother's body and to incorporate the mother's breast are repressed; instead, it is the homosexual partner's body and penis that become a substitute for the mother's breast. The homosexual's sexual contact helps the homosexual regain his masculinity by incorporating the partner's penis and masculine body.

Like Bieber et al., Socarides gave numerous examples of how the mothers of his patients had impaired the formation of their sons' normal masculine identities.

Socarides (1988, pp. 543–544) enumerated four therapeutic tasks that must be completed to treat sexual deviations successfully. He said that although these tasks are especially significant in the treatment of preoedipal perversions, they are also useful as guidelines for the treatment of oedipal perversions. These tasks are: (1) separating and disidentifying from the preoedipal mother; (2) analyzing symptoms to show their unconscious meanings; (3) providing insight into the function of the erotic experience in the perverse acts; and (4) "spoiling" the perverse gratification.

REFERENCES

BIEBER. I., Dain, J.H., Dince, P.R., Drellich, M.G., Grand, H.G., Gundlach, R.H., Kremer, M.W., Rifkin, A.H., Wilbur, C.B., Bieber, T.B. (1962). *Homosexuality: A Psychoanalytic Study*. New York: Basic Books.

FREUD, A. (1949). Some clinical remarks concerning the treatment of cases of male homosexuality. *International Journal of Psychoanalysis* 30.

———— (1951). Homosexuality Abstract:*Bulletin American Psychoanalytic Association* 7.

FREUD, S. (1905). Three essays on the theory of sexuality. *Standard Edition* 7:125–243.

———— (1916). Introductory lectures on psychoanalysis, the sexual life of human beings. *Standard Edition* 16.

———— (1920). The psychogenesis of a case of homosexuality in a woman. *Standard Edition* 18:145–172.

———— (1927). Fetishism. *Standard Edition* 21:154.

———— (1938). An outline of psychoanalysis, The psychical apparatus and the external world. *Standard Edition* 23.

FENICHEL, O. (1945). *The Psychoanalytic Theory of Neurosis*. New York: W.W. Norton and Company, Inc.

SOCARIDES, C.W. (1968). *The Overt Homosexual*. New York and London: Grune & Stratton.

———— (1988). *The Preoedipal Origin and Psychoanalytic Therapy of Sexual Perversions*. Madison, CT: International Universities Press.

WIEDEMAN, G.H. (1962). Survey of psychoanalytic literature on overt male homosexuality. *Journal of the American Psychoanalytic Association* 10:386–409.

———— (1974). Homosexuality, a survey. *Journal of the American Psychoanalytic Association* 22:651–696.

THE PSYCHOANALYTIC TREATMENT OF
AN OEDIPAL MALE HOMOSEXUAL[1]

Sexual deviations are collections of usually ego-syntonic behaviors that result from a compromise formation. They arise out of an unconscious conflict between unacceptable infantile sexual impulses and defenses against them. In all perversion there is a repetitive fixed behavior leading to orgasm. The perversion itself represents an interference by a component drive with the integration of genital sexuality.

The case that I describe here shows a milder form of oedipal homosexuality (Socarides, 1978) in which disturbances in the Oedipus complex and accompanying castration anxiety undid an integrating genital primacy. Anxiety led to preoedipal infantile sexuality because genital enjoyment had become threatening and therefore impossible. Anxiety also led to a negative oedipal position. The treatment recounted herein was successful without the use of parameters, through the psychoanalysis of the transference, dreams, fantasies, associations, and with the technique of free association. The psychoanalytic process gradually released the patient's isolated affective states, gave him insight into the genetic and psychodynamic origin of his symptoms, and led to the disappearance of homosexual and other symptoms associated with his oedipal conflicts.

CLINICAL ILLUSTRATION

Cal, an international sales executive, was a handsome, well-built, casually dressed, thirty-eight-year-old, divorced man. He sought therapy because he had difficulty choosing the right words and deciding what to say when he had important things to say to significant people. Consequently, his speech was punctuated by long pauses. This embarrassing problem had begun in childhood, and was now humiliating him at work.

Although Cal could easily talk to his employees, people younger than himself, and strangers, he became tongue-tied when speaking

---

[1]A version of this chapter was published previously in: *The Homosexualities and the Therapeutic Process,* C. Socarides and V. Volkan eds. Chapter 9, pp. 191–205. International Universities Press, Inc., 1991.

to superiors, executives, older men, large groups, close friends, or certain women. Cal had no difficulty finding words or deciding what to say when he spoke in any one of five foreign languages, nor did he have difficulty communicating in writing. Cal did not seek therapy for his homosexual behavior. This apparently was ego-syntonic and, to his mind, unalterable.

BACKGROUND

Cal was an only child, born to a fifty-year-old father and a forty-year-old mother. He remembered nothing of his early development. When he was five, his father had a heart attack and remained mostly bedridden. After that, Cal's mother often told him to be "quiet" and "good" or else his father might die. Following his father's heart attack, his mother began a prolonged affair with his father's cardiologist. She confided in Cal about this affair, but insisted that he not tell his father. Cal's father spent little time with Cal and always seemed angry, especially on those rare occasions when he was drunk. When Cal was 19, his father died of an acute infection.

Cal described his mother as a "prim and proper housewife," who was always dressed "formally" in silk stockings and high heels. Cal ate dinners with his parents in a formal candlelight setting until his father became ill. Then Cal and his mother continued to eat these formal dinners in the dining room while his father ate alone in bed upstairs. His mother insisted that Cal dress properly for these meals. Cal hated these dinners and always tried to eat alone. His mother never allowed Cal to play with the other children in the neighborhood because she considered them to be "low class." Cal's mother repeatedly attributed her chronic physical complaints to Cal's birth and delivery, and Cal feared that, if he allowed himself to get too close to other women, he might similarly harm them.

When eight, Cal was sent off to a boarding school. After that, he spent little time at home. He attended an exclusive prep school and an Ivy League university. His grades were always excellent.

Cal's homosexual activity began soon after he arrived at the boarding school and was his exclusive sexual outlet until his first year in college. Then, over a three-month period, he tried dating several girls. He was "never comfortable" with these girls. Following his father's death, Cal abruptly ceased dating and resumed having multiple, brief, homosexual encounters. In these encounters he sought sexual release, never love. His homosexual activity included oral and anal sex, and he alternately played the active and the passive role. Although he preferred the active role, he often fantasied himself to be a woman pleasing a man. Cal had an unusually high sex drive, requiring three to five orgasms per day.

When Cal was thirty, his mother became terminally ill. Shortly after that, he was pursued by a woman, Jane. Jane was the first woman he dated since early college and the first woman with whom he had sexual intercourse. After a short courtship—just before his mother died—Cal married Jane. Cal was warm and affectionate with her, but he avoided looking at her naked body and never touched her genitals with his hands. He and Jane seldom had intercourse, abstaining for periods of up to two years during their eight-year marriage. During intercourse Cal's fantasies were always homosexual. While married, although Cal did not engage in homosexual activity, he masturbated three to five times a day with homosexual fantasies. Cal eventually became convinced that he preferred homosexuality to heterosexuality, and he divorced Jane.

COURSE OF THE ANALYSIS

Shortly after that, Cal began psychoanalysis five times a week. The analysis required no parameters and lasted three and three-quarters years. For the first six months of the analysis Cal complained meekly about my passivity and tried to get me to tell him what to do. He compared my inactivity and silence to his father's feebleness and felt that my silence meant that I was critical of him.

On a business trip to Spain, he met Nancy, a "casually dressed," attractive, American woman ten years younger than himself. He found he could speak in Spanish without difficulty to Nancy. Nancy displayed interest in him, and, at her suggestion, they began a sexual relationship. It was Nancy who always initiated sexual intercourse, and Cal was surprised and pleased that she did so three to four times a day. Cal avoided looking at Nancy's "vagina" because it disgusted him.

On their return to the United States, when Cal and Nancy began conversing in English, Cal became tongue-tied with her and tried to avoid eating meals with her in a formal setting because it made him anxious. On resuming his analysis, he construed my silence to mean that I was critical of him for having had sexual intercourse with Nancy. He then became increasingly sexually inhibited with Nancy, and he avoided her by compulsively reading detective stories. During this period, homosexual fantasies inundated his thoughts, and he was driven to engage in multiple, brief sexual encounters with men. Eventually, I asked him what had led him to believe that I was critical of him for having had sexual intercourse with Nancy. Unable to summon any evidence to support his belief, Cal realized that he had felt that I was critical because, "in the back of his mind" he had a fantasy that I was jealous of his sexual relationship with Nancy. He knew there could be no truth to this fantasy because I had never seen Nancy, knew practically nothing about her, and could not, therefore, desire her sexually.

Several days later, at the end of a session, while deferentially handing me a payment check, Cal haltingly and with long pauses asked me to change an appointment time so that he could spend a weekend away with Nancy. That night, Cal dreamed: "My car would not go up a slippery ramp and I resented having to pay a mechanic to fix it."

The next day Cal admitted that at the end of the previous session he had withheld the following series of thoughts. At first he was pleased that he would be "outdoing" his analyst when he went off for the weekend to have sex with beautiful Nancy. Second, he thought that I would be jealous of him for planning this trip and would, therefore, resent being asked to change the appointment time. He then felt anger at me for apparently not wanting to change the appointment time, and he felt guilty for this anger. He defended against his anger and punished himself by doubting: He began obsessively to ruminate over what to say, how to say it, and when to say it. Cal defensively isolated this entire series of thoughts from himself and withheld them from me until the next session. Finally, to conceal his anger further, he used reaction-formation by presenting his analyst with the payment check in an overly acquiescent and subservient manor.

Upon reviewing this series of associations, Cal understood that a dream of the night before meant that he resented having to defer to (pay) his analyst (the mechanic) to fix his penis (the car) so that he could go away with Nancy and have his penis go up Nancy's slippery vagina (the ramp). This belief was a consequence of his having projected onto his analyst both his own competitive desire to have sex with Nancy and his own guilty self-critical attitude for having these competitive sexual desires for her. Cal learned that he had defensively projected onto his analyst his own unacceptable, competitively aggressive wish to outdo his analyst sexually, and imagined that his analyst was competitively jealous of his sexual activity.

This pattern of projecting his own competitiveness with his analyst, onto his analyst, was repeated often and worked through in the transference. At various times, Cal felt that his analyst was competitively jealous and critical of him (1) for having too much sex with Nancy; (2) for going away on trips to work in distant countries; (3) for overeating gourmet food; or (4) for reading entertaining detective stories instead of working. I pointed out to him that the criticism that he imagined to be coming from his analyst was similar to the criticism he had directed toward his father. Cal had criticized his father for (1) requiring too much of his mother's time; (2) spending too little time with Cal; (3) overeating; and (4) reading entertaining detective stories instead of working. With surprise, Cal acknowledged this correlation.

Cal came to understand that he had projected his own early, aggressive-competitive criticisms of his father onto the image of his father that he then transferred onto his analyst. In other words, after Cal had transferred his father image onto his analyst, Cal projected his own aggressive-competitive criticisms toward his father onto this transferred father imago. In this way, once this transference and projection had taken place, Cal had felt that the aggressive-competitive criticisms that he had originally felt toward his father were being directed toward him by his analyst.

In support of this interpretation, Cal recalled that during adolescence he had felt that his enfeebled father had envied Cal's youth and health. Cal now speculated that this could have been a projection of his own jealousy of his father's relationship with his mother onto his father. It then occurred to him that most of his homosexual fantasies contained the theme of an aggressive man "winning out" against, and "demeaning," a passive man. Cal recognized that this fantasy represented his unacceptable competitive-aggressive childhood wish to demean and depose his enfeebled father.

Next, Cal realized that he had made both his "ill, feeble" father and his "passive, ineffectual" analyst seem less delicate and vulnerable by projecting onto them his own aggressive-competitive feelings toward them. Cal had then used these contrived, frighteningly prohibitive representations of his father and his analyst to restrain and control his own feared aggressive-competitive impulses toward them. For example, Cal unrealistically exaggerated his father's anger during his drunken rages to make him seem more formidable.

Cal now understood why male authority figures whom he had initially seen as likeable, but ineffectual and weak, he later saw as autocratic, irascible, and invulnerable: He had unconsciously transferred his feeble-father imago onto these men and seen them as likeable, but powerless; later he unconsciously projected onto them his own aggressive-competitive feelings toward them and saw them as irascible and invulnerable. For example, Cal's belief that the president of the company he worked for was an irascible, dogmatic figure was a fantasy that Cal had created to protect the president from Cal's own competitive wish to be smarter, more competent, and more productive than the president.

Now that Cal was consciously aware of his own competitive-aggressiveness, he realized that he had always treated his male employees better than his female employees, not, as he had previously thought, because he preferred men, but because he had used reaction-formation against his hostile competitive feelings toward these men.

After achieving these major new insights, Cal became much less inhibited. He could then express anger directly toward his analyst, his male colleagues, and Nancy, and his dreams became openly aggressive. For example, Cal dreamed that he robbed a bank, and a policeman, who resembled his analyst, severely damaged his getaway car, so he killed the policeman. In another dream, "An older man was recommending that natural gas be socialized." Cal associated that he wished his analyst would recommend that he (the patient) "blow farts" in an aggressive masculine way. This meant that he wished his analyst would "kiss his ass" instead of his having to "kiss his analyst's ass." In a third dream, Cal aggressively pulled down a woman's pants and kissed her genitals.

His presenting symptom of obsessional doubting often appeared during his analytic sessions. For example, when I made an interpretation, instead of responding, he first fell silent, then his speech was interrupted by long pauses, his sentences became vague and confused, and his mannerisms became passive and childish. When I pointed out this behavior to him, he said he was having difficulty finding words and deciding what to say. I encouraged him to verbalize his thoughts. He said that his speech was blocked because he felt that his analyst would become angry if he told him what he was thinking, namely, that the interpretation was incorrect. He knew that the interpretation was made tentatively and that I never displayed anger toward him, but, he could never be sure that I would not get angry. Cal remembered that, when drunk, his usually docile father had flown into rages. After working through many similar episodes, it became obvious to Cal that his obsessional doubting occurred regularly, not, as he had first thought, when he feared his analyst's anger, but when he felt guilty for wanting to aggressively confront and outdo his analyst. He then recalled many past episodes in which he had become tongue-tied when he had wished to confront or outdo a male authority figure.

As Cal worked on his uncontrollable, disabling speech inhibition he recalled that, when he was a child, his mother had often told him that if he did not keep quiet, he might disturb and thereby kill his ailing father. After his mother told him this, Cal always worried he might harm his father if he spoke to him too loudly or too forcefully. This worry turned out to be an early instance of Cal's obsessional doubting and the origin of his speech inhibition. He now realized that he had been unconsciously inhibiting his speech with his analyst because he unconsciously feared that, if he aggressively confronted his usually silent analyst with words, his analyst might become even more "passive" and die.

He began to accept that he had exaggerated his father's, and then his analyst's, omnipotent invulnerability to protect them, not only from his own unconscious competitive-aggressive feelings toward them, but also from what he felt to be the magical power of his aggressive words. Then his speech inhibition gradually began to diminish. On another occasion he realized that he was forgetting the names of prominent visitors to punish himself for having unconscious aggressive-competitive feelings toward them. Now, he gradually began to have less trouble remembering names.

Cal lost fifteen pounds and bought new clothes more appropriate to his age and station. Instead of casual clothing, Cal began to wear more formal suits. He replaced his old Volkswagen with a new Porsche. He moved his keys and wallet from his back pocket to his front pocket, saying he was no longer embarrassed about "having a bulge in the front." After Nancy agreed to move in with him, he made a "fool" of himself at a party. Cal then dreamed that people jeered at him and avoided him. This "foolish" behavior and self-punitive dream brought home to him that he was guilty, and was punishing himself, for having succeeded with Nancy.

Suddenly it occurred to him that, in his usual homosexual fantasy of an aggressive man "winning out" against, and thereby "demeaning," a passive man, there was generally, somewhere in the background, an attractive woman who was intimately, but indirectly, connected with the passive man. Associating to this fantasy, my patient concluded that the aggressive man represented himself, the passive man represented his feeble father, and the attractive woman represented his mother. Having made these discoveries, Cal realized that his usual, manifestly homosexual fantasy had *always* concealed his unconscious hetero- sexual wish to have sex with the attractive woman (his mother) who was indirectly connected with the humiliated man (his father). Cal learned that in his sexual fantasies he had identified with both of his parents: Although he consciously imagined himself to be the woman (uncon- sciously his mother) sexually pleasing the man (unconsciously his father), in his unconscious he had been the man (his father) being sexu- ally pleased by the woman (his mother). It became evident to Cal that, beginning with his parents, he had concealed his heterosexual inclination and identification behind his homosexual fantasy and identification. This new insight showed that Cal's identification with his mother was a negative oedipal position rather than a preoedipal fixation. He now understood the formerly inexplicable envy he always felt toward the men with whom he had sexual encounters.

At this point Cal dreamed: "A doctor was doing plastic surgery on people to make them all look alike." He concluded that in this dream he was making men and women alike so that there would be no reason for men to compete for women.

While having intercourse with Nancy, Cal was now usually *fanta- sying* having intercourse with women other than Nancy—especially those women he had been unconsciously attracted to in adolescence. Occasionally, to have an orgasm, Cal still had to *fantasy* having sex with a man.

Cal dreamed that a feeble, but distinguished-looking old man who resembled both his father and his analyst was reproaching him for aban- doning his wife, Jane, to live with Nancy. Both Jane and Nancy looked like his mother. His associations to the dream were as follows: He had become involved with Jane after his mother became terminally ill because he feared losing his mother and wanted to have a replacement. While his mother was alive, he maintained a cool, infrequent, and restrained sexual relationship with Jane, visited his mother often, and had long affectionate conversations with her. After her death, he turned to Jane for the conversation, love, and affection that was no longer available from his mother. This substitution made him at first extremely sexually inhibited with Jane because he was guilty for having sexual feelings for a woman onto whom he had transferred his mother's role. Cal realized that the ailing old man in the dream, who resembled both his father and his analyst, represented his conscience censuring him for turning his loving and affectionate relationship with Jane (his mother) into an erotic relationship with Nancy (also his mother).

In another dream Cal was alternately being treated by two analysts. He told only his romantic thoughts to one, and only his erotic thoughts to the other. Working on dreams such as these and on his memories of his old former wife Jane and his interactions with Nancy, Cal learned that he had isolated his erotic feelings from his affectionate feelings because he did not want to know that he had had erotic feelings for his mother. He realized that he was avoiding eating dinners in a sexually seductive, intimate, formal setting with Nancy because such dinners threatened to remind him that the candlelight meals he had once had with his primped-up mother had been not only intellectually stimulating, but also sexually provocative. Cal gradually became able to be simultaneously both romantic and erotic with Nancy.

Emerging sexual desires led him to a dream of performing fellatio on his analyst. Fellatio would placate his analyst's resentment and jealousy of his new heterosexual fantasies and activities. In a similar vein, he dreamed that he was climbing up a steep cliff with another man. He felt he could get to the top if the other man could. He associated that if, unlike his father, his therapist was vigorous and could "get it (his penis) up," Cal need not feel guilty about "getting his penis up." A dream of "looking for a spicy salad dressing" led him to state that he wanted to "spice up" his life with heterosexuality.

Just before leaving on a trip, he said he experienced strong dependent feelings toward his analyst and irrationally felt his analyst was about to abandon him. He compared these feelings of frustrated longing to those he had experienced when his mother "dumped" him into a boarding school when he was eight. This was the only time during the analysis that Cal re-experienced, in the transference, anxiety related to separation from his mother. Cal quickly worked this through in the transference. He realized that he had avoided getting close to women, not only because he feared taking them away from other men and because he feared having simultaneous erotic and affectionate feelings for them, but also because he feared being abandoned by them as he felt he had been by his mother.

PRIMAL SCENE MATERIAL

Cal had a series of dreams over a period of several months that contained at least one of the following elements: (1) a man watching Cal and Nancy having intercourse; (2) two men fighting over an exotic spice shop (a woman); (3) the Mafia trying to "get" him because he killed the Godfather; (4) coming to his session, Cal finds his analyst is not there, so Cal climbs into bed with his analyst's wife; (5) Cal is observing two people having intercourse (a) through a balcony railing, (b) through a net, or (c) through a wall; (6) Cal is surprised by a light shining through a window that reveals a crime in progress; (7) Cal is in a wire shopping basket watching a "black kid shoving something up a white kid's ass." To the dream elements "balcony railing" and "wire shopping basket" Cal associated a baby crib.

From Cal's associations to these dreams the analyst suggested the following reconstruction: While watching through the railing of his crib, Cal observed his parents having sexual intercourse. This spectacle excited him and led him to make noise that disturbed and angered his parents. This experience frightened Cal and led to his heterosexual inhibition.

Reconstruction of the primal scene (Freud, 1939) was supported and refined by work on two subsequent dreams. In the first dream Cal was watching a man having intercourse with a woman: Cal could see that she had no penis. In the second dream while Cal was watching a man have intercourse with a woman: Cal wanted to reach out and touch the woman's genitals, but the man became angry. To these two dreams Cal associated that, if he had interrupted his parents while they were having intercourse and had noted that his mother had no penis, he might have fantasied that his father had cut his mother's penis off. Cal could then have further fantasied that his angered father could cut Cal's penis off for interrupting intercourse. Cal might then have fantasied appeasing his angered father, by presenting his anus for intercourse. This could explain, in part, the origin of Cal's homosexual predilection.

Following these new insights, Cal dreamed that he was in his analyst's bedroom with his analyst. Nancy walked in, but Cal could not introduce his analyst to Nancy because he could neither speak nor think of his analyst's name. He realized that his inhibition in the dream expressed his hostile wish to keep his analyst away from Nancy. Cal then had other dreams that further convinced him that the origin of his speech and his heterosexual inhibition was caused by his oedipal conflict. Once he understood that he avoided looking at Nancy's genitals because her lack of a penis reminded him that he could lose his penis, Cal became able to look at her genitals without disgust. Cal and Nancy then planned to get married.

As his psychoanalysis proceeded, Cal became more productive at work, and earned several promotions. Eventually, he received an offer to manage another company in a distant city. This job would allow him to do many things he had wanted to do, but could not do because of his inhibitions. More work had been achieved in his analysis than he had anticipated, and we agreed that he would terminate the analysis in eight months so that he could accept this new position.

Cal did not relapse with these successes as he would have in the past. Instead, he had dreams that showed that he did not want to interrupt the analysis: In one, the water ran out of his tub before he finished taking his bath. In another, his analyst was a devil, whom Cal blamed for not "pulling everything together." In a third Cal was "gay," which "proved" he was not ready to terminate. In these dreams, Cal recognized his dependent wish to remain in analysis, but he also knew that he had overcome his speech and sexual inhibitions and that he was ready and able to be on his own. Undisguised dreams, corroborating what Cal had already learned about his unconscious fears, guilt, and needs, were now occurring almost daily.

During the analysis, as Cal became able to express his anger toward his analyst more openly, he became less inhibited and more comfortable when speaking to superiors, important executives, older men, large groups, close friends, and women. He had also become more friendly with both men and women, and could enjoy the power and prestige that his achievements warranted. His sexual fantasies had gradually changed from his observing an aggressive man "winning out" against, and thereby "demeaning," a passive man (who was intimately, but indirectly, connected with an attractive woman), to his having sexual relations with a woman other than Nancy, to his having sex with Nancy. Eventually, Cal ceased having homosexual fantasies entirely, and he became able, without anxiety, to kiss Nancy, look at her genitals, and talk intellectually, seriously, and tenderly to her about their relationship. Cal had come to see that his homosexual fantasies and activities had defensively served to interpose his father between himself and his mother.

DISCUSSION

Cal's pathological, unconscious intrapsychic conflict began, when he was five years old, following his father's heart attack and the beginning of his mother's affair with his father's cardiologist. These two traumatic experiences reinforced Cal's presumed earlier traumatic experience of the primal scene. They produced intense castration anxiety that led to the development of the following defense mechanisms against both his aggressive-competitive feelings toward his father and his sexual desires for his mother:

1. *Projection* of his own unacceptable, aggressive-competitive wish to take his father's place with his mother onto his father. He then imagined that his father was competitively jealous of Cal's closeness to his mother. This projection furthermore unconsciously protected his father from Cal's aggression by making his father seem indomitable and invulnerable.

2. After his mother told Cal that he might cause his father to die if he spoke too loudly or too aggressively, he unconsciously inhibited his speech by *obsessional doubting*. This was the basis of the symptom for which he initially came for treatment: a difficulty in remembering what to say, deciding what to say, and how to say it.

3. *Reaction-formation* to conceal his aggressive-competitive feelings toward his father. This made him acquiescent, subservient, passive, and effeminate toward his father and later toward other males.

4. *Isolation* of his erotic feelings from his thoughts of his mother.

In this patient there was a failure of resolution of the Oedipus complex; castration fears led to a negative oedipal position. He suffered from a *structural conflict* between major structures of the ego, id, and superego, that is, between his aggressive, sexual and other wishes, and his guilt and ideals. His nuclear conflict consisted of a renunciation of oedipal love for his mother. This is in contrast to preoedipally fixated homosexual patients who suffer from an object relations class of conflict: that is, anxiety and guilt associated with the failure of development in the phase of self-object differentiation (Socarides, 1978). In the latter case, we would have to deal more with nuclear conflicts that consist of desire for and dread of merging with the mother in order to reinstate the primitive mother-child unity with its associated separation and/or fragmentation anxiety (Socarides, 1978). Fortunately, the status of ego function in my patient, including his object relations, were relatively intact.

Because Cal's illness was of the oedipal form, little work needed to be done in the analysis to facilitate the process of self-object differentiation and separation and disidentifying from the preoedipal mother. However, anxieties relating to separation from the mother were present. It was the separation anxiety that emerged when his mother became terminally ill, which led him to turn immediately to Jane, a substitute heterosexual object, for the love and support he knew he was about to lose. Once during the analysis, after he had regressed into the mother transference, Cal experienced similar separation anxiety. Just before leaving on a prolonged business trip, he developed a feeling of frustrated longing and said that he unrealistically feared that his analyst was about to abandon him. Immediately and without difficulty he recognized and worked through that this feeling was similar to the way he felt when his mother had sent him away to boarding school.

Decoding or analyzing the unconscious meaning of the perverse symptom was accomplished through the analysis of Cal's transference to his analyst. The patient noticed himself assuming a passive, effeminate role toward the analyst and, simultaneously, observed himself becoming irrationally convinced that his analyst was competitively jealous of Cal's sexual activities. He learned that this feeling was a result of his having defensively projected onto his analyst his own unacceptable, competitively-aggressive wishes to outdo his analyst sexually.

He next recalled that as a child he had hidden his own aggressive-competitive heterosexual inclinations behind passive homosexual fantasies and activities while simultaneously projecting these same inclinations onto his father. Through this projection, Cal had unrealistically exaggerated both his analyst's and his father's strength and potency, thus protecting them from what Cal imagined to be the destructive magical power of his own competitive-aggressive inclinations. This process was re-enacted in the transference and interpreted. Cal also observed in the transference that he was using his speech inhibition to protect his analyst from what he felt to be the destructive magical power of his hostile aggressive words. He then remembered that his speech inhibition began when his mother told him not to be "noisy" or his father would "die."

The fourth task, which involves the "spoiling" of the perversion—altering the pleasure associated with the sexually deviant acts—occurred gradually throughout the treatment, spontaneously and without the use of parameters or prohibition, in any sense, of the sexual acts. Once the meaning of the unconscious fantasy system hidden behind his deviant acts was uncovered (decoded) and made conscious through the process of the analysis, Cal began to notice a decrease in his sexual desire to arouse himself by fantasies of, or sex with, men.

This paper shows that a patient suffering from the oedipal form of homosexuality is an ideal candidate for successful psychoanalytic treatment of this disorder.

REFERENCES

FREUD, S. (1927). Fetishism. *Standard Edition,* 21:149–157. London: Hogarth Press, 1961.

——— (1939). Moses and Monotheism: Three Essays. *Standard Edition,* 23:78–80. London: Hogarth Press, 1964.

SOCARIDES, C.W. (1978). *Homosexuality.* New York: Jason Aronson, Inc.

——— (1979). A Unitary Theory of Sexual Perversion. In: *On Sexuality: Psychoanalytic Observations.* Eds. T.P. Karasu and C.W. Socarides. New York: International Universities Press. pp. 161–188.

——— (1988). *The Preoedipal Origin and Psychoanalytic Therapy of Sexual Perversions.* Madison, CT: International Universities Press, 543–544.

THE METAMORPHOSIS OF A HOMOSEXUAL MAN

This chapter reports on the psychoanalytic treatment of a homosexual patient. The report recounts the session-by-session course of therapy, the chronological development and resolution of the transference neurosis, the patient's psychodynamics, the childhood and latency determinants of the patient's castration and separation anxiety, and the subsequent manifestations of his separation and castration anxiety.

Pete was a forty-year-old, tall, well built, well dressed, noneffeminate-appearing, homosexual man. His major complaint was "lifelong anxiety" that recently manifested as a "fear that he might have AIDS." His other complaints were "stomach pains," "back pains," a "feeling of incompleteness," an "inability to express feelings," and a "fear of becoming too aggressive." Pete had been in one or another form of psychotherapy—including eight years of psychoanalysis—since he was eighteen-years-old. None of these therapies had relieved his symptoms.

PRESENTING HISTORY

Pete's mother told him that she already had a two-year-old son, so she got pregnant a second time to get a girl. This pregnancy turned out to be another boy, Pete. When Pete was three years old, his sister was born. His mother then turned all her attention to his sister, and he felt "devastated." He tried to regain his mother's attention and approval by giving her small gifts and dressing like a girl. She did not object when he put on her clothing and she "continued to ignore" him. Pete said that, at about the age of five, he stopped trying to "win back" his mother, "withdrew from the family," and "resolved never to become dependant on anyone again." When he was old enough, he avoided his parents and siblings by moving into the basement, eating alone, and washing his own clothing.

Pete's parents displayed no affection for each other and argued frequently. His mother seemed to win these arguments, because his father would back off and leave the house. After his father left, his mother would tell Pete how bad his father was. In an effort to regain the "attention and approval" that he had lost when his sister was born, Pete supported his mother's opinion of his father. He tried to be as unlike his father as he could, and he soon became his mother's "intimate, intellectual confidant." Pete was afraid that his father might, "without warning, beat him up for this." Later, in kindergarten, Pete feared that the boys might "without warning, beat him up," so he only played with girls. During latency, his mother took him "instead of" his father to concerts and plays. Pete feared his father would object, but his father never did. Because his parents never shut their bedroom door, he believed that they never had intercourse.

In puberty, Pete began to masturbate with the fantasy that he was playing a passive, receptive, feminine role with an "aggressive, beefy older man." At this same time, he began to argue with his mother and stopped being her confidant. At 16, Pete began "cruising the street to pick up men for sex." He preferred "married men with large penises." He would ejaculate when these men ejaculated into either his mouth or his anus. If he "even had the thought of penetrating them," he would lose his erection.

In high school Pete "avoided athletics, and clowned around to make people happy." He became class president. Throughout his schooling, he always got top grades, and he earned a Ph.D.

Pete had many affectionate, long-term, platonic relationships with women, but never with men. One time Pete tried, but failed, to form an affectionate, monogamous, long-term, sexual relationship with a man. However, this man was frequently unfaithful. Eventually this man stole Pete's money, and left him.

SUMMARY OF PROCESS NOTES
AND COURSE OF THERAPY

The following summaries of Pete's psychoanalytic sessions (from notes numbered 1 through 1897) detail the development of Pete's progressive insight into the unconscious determinants of his homosexual behavior. The patient's remarks, or paraphrased remarks, are enclosed in quotation marks. Descriptions of his dreams are italicized. He would often recall an unconscious determinant, re-repress it, and then re-remember it.

4. Between the ages of five and eight, Pete had a recurrent nightmare: *"A snake was coming out of a cupboard to bite my mother."* He said that his previous psychoanalyst had told him that the snake represented his father's penis. I asked if the snake might also represent Pete's penis. He replied that this could be true because he had always tried to "hide his penis" so that he "would not reveal too much aggression." He added that, when I had enquired about his sexual history, he had felt like I was demanding to see his penis. Pete then recalled that his mother had ridiculed him in front of her friends by telling them that when he was two and one half, a woman on the beach had tried to help him take off his bathing suit, and he had yelled angrily, "No! No! That's mine!"

18. When I told Pete that he had been late to several of our sessions, he replied that he was pleased that I noticed. He said that it made him feel that I was a strong, aggressive man who cared about him.

32. Pete said, "There's something freeing about recognizing that I need to be dominated by a strong man in order to have sexual feelings. However, it's also very frightening—because it means that I might be able to have sex without needing a strong man. I don't remember ever loving anyone, but I must have loved my mother because, between the ages of three and five, I spent what little money I had buying her gifts. When five, I wanted to join the Cub Scouts, but my mother said, 'No, all you want is the uniform.' So I swallowed my wish to be a cub scout, kept it all inside, and got my stomach cramps. That was the only time I asked her to let me do something masculine, and her message was a clear 'No.' So, after that, I played only with girls and mother never objected. After that, I never joined any male group, never did sports, and never got into fights. I envied men who could do those things. My mother had one daughter! Why did she need two? I couldn't imagine letting her know that I had a penis. My father wasn't there to protect me from her, so I developed stomach cramps and sought protection from male doctors. I felt that my father's absence meant that he wanted me to marry his wife. At five, I saw my father in his boxer shorts and I became sexually excited. I then would secretly put them on and play with my penis."

37. "After my sister was born, I pretended I didn't have a penis, in hopes of regaining my mother's love. Since that time, I have feared that someone would find out that I have a penis. Now, when I lecture in front of a group, I wear several jock straps to conceal my penis. I'm furious that my mother would not let me be a boy. She even objected to my sucking my thumb and put pepper on it. So I became stuck and

frozen. My mother's sister noticed that I only played with girls, and she told my mother that I should see a psychiatrist, but my mother said it was 'only a phase.'"

39. One week after beginning his psychoanalysis, Pete became sexually involved with Don. Don had just "come-out" as homosexual and had divorced his wife. Don had played college football, was masculine in appearance, and could play the "top-man" role for Pete. Don, however, preferred to play the "bottom-man" role, and wanted Pete to enter his anus. Pete could not.

55. Pete says he wants me to tell him to stop his close relationship with Don like he had wanted his father to tell him to stop his close relationship to his mother. However, when his previous psychoanalyst told him to stop his homosexual activity, he continued the activity without telling his analyst.

56. Dream: "*A woman was chasing me. I was terrified. She took my calendar, my appointment book, and a curved stick about six-inches long.*" Associations: "Last night I tried to enter Don's anus, but I became *terrified*, and lost my erection. Then I felt compelled to go out and seek anonymous sex from a stranger. The *woman chasing me* in the dream represented both Don and my mother. The *calendar, appointment book, and curved stick six inches long* represented my penis. My dream meant that if I were to become sexually aggressive with anyone, that person would *take* my penis."

63. "In the second grade a boy told me that if you get an erection with a nurse, she will hit it with a pencil. That thought makes me angry. I'm beginning to think that I dread castration. I doubt that my mother ever threatened to castrate me, but I did wish that my father had been there to protect me from her. I still need a strong man to protect me. I can't believe that Don, unlike my mother, wants me to use my penis aggressively."

64. "When my former analyst pushed me to try sex with a woman, I couldn't. Now, without your pushing I've stayed in a relationship with Don, a bottom-man. I can walk around naked with him and sleep with him. Never before was I even able to do that."

69. Pete criticized me for making him stand and wait by the couch while I put down a head-towel. It made him feel awkward. I did not change my routine, and he continued to complain. I asked if he was arguing with me to distance himself from me—like he had argued with his mother to distance himself from her. He saw that he was and added that

no matter how I had responded to his complaint, he would have distanced himself from me. He had pulled away because he was irritated that I had not changed my towel routine. However, if I had changed my routine, he would have pulled away because he would have become afraid of his own aggression. Pete then recounted other instances when he had done the same thing with others including his former psychotherapists.

72. The prior session, Pete had recognized and talked about how he had been projecting his mother's rejection of his masculinity onto both Don and me. Following this session, Pete, for the first time, was able to ejaculate into a man's—Don's—mouth. Afterward, Pete felt that both Don and I would criticize him for doing so, but he immediately realized that he was transferring his mother's negative attitude toward his masculine aggressiveness onto both of us. He said that, when his former analyst told him that his cruising was acting out, and that he should stop cruising and direct his sexual desires toward his analyst, Pete felt that his former analyst was telling him that he should not enjoy himself, the way his mother had told him not to enjoy himself.

80. Pete said, "I have been hiding my penis my whole life because my mother wouldn't accept it. I'm angry with her for that. My homosexuality, the core of what I am, is an indirect expression of that anger. I fear that if I were to give up that anger, I might become assertive, direct my sexual needs toward another person, and get rejected again. This is the first time in my life that I have felt that it would be unpleasant to have a man put his penis into my anus. I feel it would take away my masculinity, and that makes me angry."

84. "My being with Don is the first long-term sexual relationship that I've ever had, and I want to end it. I would like to blame you for wanting me to leave him so that I could date women, but you have not said so. My first analyst pushed me to date women, and I held him responsible for my thoughts of dating women. Now, the thought, of my dating women, came from within me. Last year, I spent $7,700 for internists and almost $4000 for medication. Most of my symptoms were due to anxiety. My psychoanalysis is now saving me money. To me a football helmet and a condom are similar protective devices. One protects you from competitive-aggression, and the other protects you from sexual-aggression. My mother robbed me of my masculinity. I could scream at her for that! I fear my aggression, swallow it, and then I get stomachaches."

86. "My desire to have a man penetrate my anus is fading, but if I were to enter someone, I would feel like I was angrily beating him.

If I gave up that anger, I would become vulnerable to rejection. When I masturbate, I fantasy that I'm with a powerful, aggressive man. I can't fantasy myself being a powerful, aggressive man with anyone, because I feel that my masculine aggressiveness would be rejected—like it was by my mother."

88. "I've always been attracted to men who have big pectoral muscles and big nipples. However, today I found myself staring at a woman's breasts. I don't like where my thoughts are going. I would like to blame you, but you didn't make me stare at her breasts."

89. "I saw two women whose breasts were partly exposed. I thought, 'I'll be damned if I'll respond to that.' Did I stop myself from responding so that I wouldn't be rejected? My homosexuality may be a defense against my responding to my mother sexually."

91. "I'm afraid of committing to Don because I don't want to become vulnerable again like I was with my mother. I would rather 'withdraw and suck my thumb,' but my mother wouldn't even let me do that—so I just become anxious and inhibited. My mother wouldn't allow me to do anything fun. She didn't let me suck my thumb, or become a cub scout. My father wasn't strong enough to protect me from her, so I've spent the rest of my life looking for a man who was strong enough. I'm not sure that you are strong enough to protect me. With you I feel helpless and dependent like I did with my mother. I don't like where this psychoanalysis is going."

93. "With my mother I had friendship without sex. With men, I have sex without friendship."

96. Dream: "*I was looking up under someone's shorts. I couldn't tell whether it was a man or a woman.*" Associations: "I was looking for a penis, something that would make me unafraid, but I couldn't find it. My mother often wore short shorts."

100. "This week, each time while coming here, I had the irrational fear that I might lose control and either urinate or defecate on your couch. So, before I came into your office, I went into your bathroom and tried to empty my bladder and bowels. Whenever I go to the toilet, even just to piss, I sit down, lean forward, and push my penis down. My mother made me to do that. She got furious if I stood up to urinate because I might miss the toilet and wet the floor. That, too, was anti-male. My mother wouldn't let me suck my thumb, play boys' games, become a cub scout, or stand up to urinate. Perhaps I fear becoming incontinent on your couch because free-association is fun and you don't limit it."

107. "Don wants to feed me, take care of me, and have me penetrate his anus, but I fear that if I come to rely on him, he will reject me like my mother did." I tell him that, with Don, he has been alternating between playing the role of himself as a vulnerable, helpless, little boy and the role of his rejecting mother.

115. "When my mother stopped me from having pleasure, it was like her saying, 'You can't have pleasure with me.' So, whenever I try to enter a man's anus, the man becomes my mother, and I lose my erection. I don't want all this to be true. It makes me very uncomfortable. A strange thing happened yesterday. I tried to masturbate using my usual fantasy of having a strong man penetrate my anus, but the fantasy didn't work. . . . . . What you said is true, when I stop Don from having pleasure, I'm doing to him what my mother did to me."

119. "Yesterday, I was talking to a group of women. I felt that they were staring at my crotch instead of listening. Did I want them to look? . . . I felt like changing my clothes before coming to your office so that my penis wouldn't show."

120. "When Don and I have sex, I feel that he thinks that I'm doing something wrong, bad, and dirty. That's putting my mother onto him again. When I have anonymous sex with strangers, I don't feel that way. I make myself feel like a helpless woman to protect myself from feeling like an aggressive, potent man who is vulnerable to rejection or castration. As a kid, I feared my aggressive, masculine impulses toward my mother. My father wasn't there to stop me, so I cruised and sought a powerful father figure who would stop me."

122. "Driving here today, I saw two women and thought that they were attractive. That never happens. Where is this analysis taking me?"

124. "Last night I was able to penetrate Don's anus and ejaculate. Seeing you as a friend, enabled me to see Don as a friend, so I could do it. This was the first time I was able to penetrate anyone's anus. While doing it, I thought, 'You're mine now, and you can't leave me.' Fleetingly, I fantasied that I was in a vagina. I must confuse the rectal and the vaginal openings."

134. "For the first time I looked in a catalog at pictures of women wearing underwear. Then, I became confused and anxious. I began looking at women after I got positive feelings toward you. I went to a gay meeting and felt that I didn't belong anymore. It's weird."

145. Dream: *"Someone was ripping off my pants to get at my genitals. I awoke screaming."*

149. "I'm having trouble masturbating to orgasm. I fantasy men, then women, then men. Neither is working."

155. Don became jealous and demanded that Pete take down his photographs of nude men. Pete refused. He felt that Don's demand was like his mother's demand that he not suck his thumb or masturbate. He recognizes that he is doing to Don what Pete's mother had done to him. Pete says, "The excitement of cruising is an expression of the anger connected with the feeling: 'I will have a penis!'"

159. "Don has given up on me and plans to leave me because I can't enter him anally and play the top-man role for him. He no longer looks at me adoringly. I feel awful. However, I fear that I will lose my penis if I enter him anally. My current feeling of loss must be intensified by the feelings I had when my sister was born, and I lost my close relationship with my mother."

Pete experiences castration anxiety when Don is with him and separation anxiety when Don is not with him.

217. "Yesterday when I said you were cute, I was cruising you. I have to be careful about doing that. When my first psychoanalyst told me to stop cruising, I felt he was encouraging me to have sexual feelings for him."

218. One of Pete's woman friends, with whom he had a long-term platonic relationship, has lost 100 pounds. He says that he fears that he "might get sexual feelings for her."

220. "I became sexually aggressive with Don. That's what he wanted. If I were able to change roles that way, would I want to do that with him—or with a woman?"

222. "I'm most attracted to married men because they are strong enough to have sex with women and still keep their penises."

224. I asked Pete if his mother had ever been seductive. He replied that at times she wore "attractive halter tops and short shorts." Thinking of this made him feel "anxious and inhibited."

228. "I can't stand perfume, but I liked the smell of it coming from your wife's office. She is so nice when she greets me. Am I getting a positive mother transference toward her?"

232. Now that Don is leaving him, Pete is getting stomach pains and is trying to win Don back with small gifts. Pete realizes that he got similar stomach pains and tried to win his mother back with small gifts after she left him to care for his newborn sister.

242. Pete now begins to have a few fantasies of aggressively castrating or killing men.

244. He would like to "blame his heterosexual dreams" on me, but knows that they are his dreams.

256. Pete says that now, coming to see me is like cruising to avoid his positive feelings for Don. Pete has thoughts of kissing me. He thinks he must have begun to cruise to mitigate his positive feelings toward his mother.

257. Pete says, "While having sex with Don, right before my eyes, he became a woman with breasts and a vagina. When I ejaculated, he turned into my mother. I'm going crazy. I don't want to hallucinate that I'm having sex with my mother! It's frightening. I won't let a woman be attractive to me! No! No! No! I can't believe that Don won't become rejecting and castrating like my mother. Today, I again found myself staring at a woman. I don't want to be attracted to women, because I could then again become helpless and vulnerable to loss like I was with my mother."

263. "It frightens me to think that I could choose to be heterosexual. I don't want to stop disliking women!"

266. "Ever since Don became a woman with breasts and a vagina and turned into my mother, I've been impotent. On mothers' day, I sent flowers to my mother. I haven't done anything like that since I was five years old."

268. Tearfully, Pete says, "I saw a woman wearing a frilly, ruffled, feminine, see-through blouse. Simultaneously, I found her both attractive and disgusting. I immediately cruised for a strong man."

274. "When my sister was born, my mother displaced her attention away from me onto her. I felt destitute. I believed it was because I was not a girl. I turned to father, but he wasn't there. To win my mother back, I offered her gifts. That didn't work, so I eventually gave up and vowed never to become dependant on anyone again. In adolescence, I began to need sex. Because mother had rejected me for not being a girl, I believed that all other women would reject me for not being a girl. So I turned to, and sought, father figures for sexual gratification. I'm frightened of how angry this makes me feel."

286. "Now that Don is leaving me, I'm experiencing the terror that I must have felt when my mother left me. When I then turned to father, and he wasn't there, I almost left reality and believed that I was a girl. Cruising doesn't seem to work anymore. I want you to tell me that you will protect me and that I can be masculine and have a penis. I can't

risk believing that some women aren't like my mother. My penis shrinks when I think of having sex with a woman."

310. "When I was about five, because my mother rejected my masculinity, devalued my father, and had rejected me for my sister, I wondered if my father still had a penis. So I put on his shorts and fantasied that, like me, his penis was hidden behind them. Later, I cruised to verify that father figures—especially married father figures—still had penises. Perhaps if I had seen my father's penis, I wouldn't have had to cruise."

334. "I bought some boxer shorts and joined a gay gym. Things I have always avoided. It might alienate all my friends. I hope to lose weight and relieve my back pains. Women have been my confidants, but if I think of them as lovers, I think, 'Let them all go to hell!'"

336. Dream: *"A woman tries to seduce me. I kiss her, and put my hand into her pants."* Association: "I never had a dream like that before. Following the dream, I had to protect myself by staring at men's crotches."

337. "I'm not able to have sex with Don, and I can't find a fantasy that allows me to masturbate to orgasm. I wish I could cruise to get rid of my thoughts of women. I have really regressed back to being masculine. I'm a lousy homosexual."

339. "I want to fight with you and say, 'You can't make me heterosexual,' but you haven't tried to."

350. "My mother wouldn't accept my penis, so I ran away from her and sought father figures who would."

357. Dream: *"The elevator wouldn't go up—only down. An elevator repairman said, 'rent one, don't own one.'"* Associations: "If the *elevator* is my penis, *going up* is an erection and going down is impotence. *Renting one* is cruising for anonymous sex and *owning one* is having a relationship."

360. Dream: *"I'm trying to get a splinter out of my anus."* Associations: "The *splinter* in *my anus* is a penis. The only time my father and I worked together was when he took a *splinter out of my* finger. Since then, I have enjoyed going to male doctors."

372. Dream: *"I was in bed kissing my way up a woman's legs toward her genitals. I woke up thinking, 'Why am I doing this?'* I wanted to blame you, but the dream was mine."

381. "Last night, while playing with Don's nipples, I wondered if it would be better with a woman. Then, to ejaculate, I fantasied that some man was having sex with a woman. It was like having a father show me how."

382. "I saw a woman with large breasts and became frightened that I could become vulnerable to rejection. Sex with men is becoming less interesting, but I fear women."

391. "I'm becoming curious about straight sex. I watched a porno film of a couple fucking to see if I could get off, but I only become angry with the woman. To me fucking and hostility seem the same. I would like to learn from straight men how to live with women without being frustrated or hurt. I came here to get over my anxiety, but now I'm so anxious that when I don't have to work, I have to hide in bed all day."

408. "I can't accept that we are working together. Fighting with you would be easier. That's weird, because I have spent most of my life looking for a caring daddy. It's a big jump for me to think that I didn't get love from my father because I wouldn't accept it."

420. Dream: "*I was trying to pee into a bathtub, but I couldn't push my penis down, and I sprayed the wall.* I woke up and found that I had wet my bed. That's never happened before." Associations: "When my male cat, whom I loved and who loved me, began to *spray the wall*, I had to castrate him. When I was little, my mother made me sit down on the toilet, like a girl, and *push my penis down,* so that I wouldn't *spray* outside the toilet." [I ask if he had been enuretic as a child. He could not remember and said that he did not want to ask his parents because his father would not remember, and his mother would infuriate him by evading his question.]

423. He told me that he had phoned his mother and asked her whether he had been enuretic. She infuriated him by evading his question for more than 30 minutes. Finally, she told him that he had stopped wetting his bed when he was about two, but had resumed wetting it just after his sister was born. That night he Dreamed: "*I was at a dentist without any anesthesia.*" Associations: "Being in psychoanalysis is like being at a dentist without any anesthesia. Talking to my mother took me back to an experience I don't want to relive, and I'm angry at you for asking me to do it. Like my father, you don't help! Since I called my mother, all I can think of is cruising. Cruising is distancing. You can't get rejected if you pull back far enough. Calling my mother broke my childhood resolve that I would never again ask her for anything."

438. Dream: "*I was standing next to my mother. Pee* [urine] *was on the floor. She told me to clean it up. I said, 'No! I want to feed my cat instead.'*" Associations: "When *my cat* went into heat and began spraying my walls, I was forced to castrate him. In the dream *my cat*

represents me. Refusing to *clean up* the *pee on the floor* for *my mother* means both refusing to stop wetting my bed and refusing to emasculate myself by sitting down on the toilet and pushing my penis down to urinate. *Wanting to feed my cat instead* means that I wanted my mother to *feed* me instead of emasculating me."

441. Dreams: I. *"I was with a woman who was dressed like my mother. We were going to take an airplane flight, but I couldn't find my suitcase. I either had to give up flying with the woman or give up my suitcase."* Associations: *"I had to give up either my mother or my penis."* II: *"I was a bulky weight-lifter fighting a war."* Associations: *"I never had an aggressive dream like that before."*

462. ". . . I noticed that even at her age, my mother has a good figure, nice legs and dresses attractively. I don't like where my free associations are going."

463. "I met an intelligent, attractive, seductive, lady, Zelda, and I complimented her clothing. I never do anything like that. Afterwards, I became frightened and angry, and I had a strong urge to cruise. Later, I found myself daydreaming that I was telling her the ground rules she would have to follow if we got married and had children."

468. "I found myself staring up a woman-friend's skirt and scared the shit out of myself."

476. "Working out at the gym, I've lost 35 pounds, and my back pains are gone."

504. "I can now have an orgasm while fantasying getting a blow job from either a man or a woman, but if I fantasy putting my penis into either an anus or a vagina, I become impotent. I now realize that when cruising, I have sought more than an orgasm. I also needed to alleviate my terror by verifying that men, especially bisexual men, still had penises."

512. "In college I had sex with Phyllis several times. She was the only woman I was not afraid to have sex with. I think that she didn't scare me because she was the opposite of my mother in every way, she was actually crazy. There was no commitment. None of my women friends have been like my mother. Men are even less like her."

530. "I'm past denying that I'm lonely, but I freeze [become anxious and inhibited] at the thought of establishing a loving relationship with anyone."

537. "Yesterday, I had a fleeting thought of having sex with a woman friend."

540. He found a woman attractive who was wearing a short skirt and became frightened.

549. "My former analyst pushed me to date women and I refused. Now, from within myself, I feel a faint urge to do so, not for sex, but out of loneliness."

571. "Because my mother sided with me against my father, I became frightened and withdrew from them both."

577. "I've always envied men who can be aggressive. I hoped to gain their strength by submitting to them sexually."

582. "Last night, why did I Dream that *I was in bed with a woman* and not that I was in a bed with a man?"

590. "When I was five, I felt abandoned by my mother, and I vowed never again to become dependant on anyone again. Instead, I became like her. I'm now regressing back to thinking of becoming dependant on a woman."

592. "To overcome my mother's objection to my enjoying my penis I sought support and protection from my father, but he was too weak and would retreat from her and leave the house. Then, in puberty, when my sex drive increased, I sought protection and support from large, powerful looking, preferably married, men. I was curious about their penises and wanted them to give their penises to me in my anus. That verified that they still had penises and allowed me to ejaculate. Why won't you encourage me to enjoy my penis aggressively?"

[When Pete was a small child, because his mother would not accept his or his father's aggressive, masculine behavior, Pete became terrified that if he displayed any masculinity, he would lose his penis, as he believed his sister had lost hers. When he saw his father withdraw from the shouting matches he had with Pete's mother, Pete wondered if his father still had his penis. Pete wanted to find out, but his father never removed his undershorts, and Pete never could see the bulge of a penis under his father's undershorts. Pete put on his father's undershorts to see if he could see his own penis bulge. His penis was hidden behind his father's shorts and that meant that his father's penis was only hidden and not removed.]

602. "Zelda asked me to dinner. If I continue my analysis, I fear I might change. If she makes a pass at me, I can protect myself by telling her that I'm gay."

606. While Pete was living with and sleeping with Don, he often woke up, kicking, screaming, and terrified. He could not remember

having had a dream. Last night, however, he woke up kicking, screaming, and terrified and remembered the following dream: *"My mother
was coming into the bedroom to harm me."* Association: "I don't know
what she was going to do to me."

625. Zelda hugged him. It felt good, but frightened him.

652. "I'm terrified that I might become dependent on you and,
therefore, vulnerable to rejection, like I was with my parents. I don't
know if I'm turning you into the strong father I never had or into the
perfect mother."

659. "I'm now cruising less. When I see a big, long, prick, I wonder
why I ever cared. Neither gay nor straight porno films turn me on.
However, the thought of having sex with someone who doesn't have a
penis is terrifying. When I was 18, a girl, M, got on top of me and
talked me into sex. I can't remember what happened, but immediately
afterwards I felt compelled to go cruising for a man. I may be pressured
to have sex with men because I fear sex with women. If I wasn't afraid,
I wouldn't need a man to protect me. My reaction to sex with a woman
is half fear and half fury. I felt like that when I was with Don. I now have
faint thoughts of being on top."

666. "I fantasy arguing with Zelda. That's how I separated myself
from my mother. I hate to admit that I don't like being alone."

675. "I separate sex from friendship and cruise penises, not persons."
[He is beginning to recognize that he isolates his sexual feelings from
his affectionate feelings.]

735. "I had an unprecedented fantasy: I was a sexy male in shorts
and a T shirt."

743. "I have love feelings for you, and I fear getting an erection in
here. I both fear that you might criticize me for having these feelings
and that you might reciprocate my feelings."

748. He says that his impulse to argue with me might be a wish to
repeat the scenario of his having pushed his parents out of his life and
then blaming them for it.

767. "Yesterday, I had warm feelings toward your wife. It began
when I saw her walk by. The feelings were erotic, disgusting, and terrifying. I'm freaked out by the thought that I was sexually attracted to
my mother before she terrified me by psychologically abandoning and
emasculating me. I would like to believe that I'm making all this up, but
my feelings of fury and terror are real! It scares the living shit out of me
to experience attraction to your wife, and to my mother again. I hate to

think that my homosexuality might be the result of this and that I might have a spark of heterosexual libido."

771. Dreams: I. *"I'm running for a touchdown"* II. *"I'm in a shower sucking on a woman's breast."* He understands the meaning of the dreams instantly and is disappointed that I do not compliment him for these dreams.

846. He plans to go on a trip with a woman friend. She knows that he is gay, so they planned to save money by sharing a room. Yesterday however, she took hold of his arm. It made him anxious, so he decided to have separate rooms.

854. Pete tells me that many gay men idealize Judy Garland. When they want to find homosexual sex they say, "Let's go find Dorothy." We work on this and conclude that homosexual men revere Judy Garland because in the 1939 movie, *The Wizard of Oz*, she helped three incomplete males try to gain their missing masculine attributes: She helped the Straw Man seek a brain, the Tin Man seek a heart, and the Cowardly Lion seek courage. She, thus, is the antithesis of Pete's mother, who, to him, seemed to object to his masculine attributes. Like Pete, these three flawed males "cruised" the Yellow Brick Road in search of an idealized, powerful, Big-Daddy-Wizard who would give them their missing masculine attributes. However, when they found the Wizard, he turned out to be a phony, powerless, pretentious, faker, who told them that they already had the masculine attributes that they thought they lacked.[1]

873. "Yesterday, because you spoke a lot, you became what I look for when I cruise—a strong, aggressive, masculine, top-man. I felt cared for, supported, and safe, and I became less afraid to be aggressive and have my penis show. However, when I began to have positive feelings toward you, I felt, 'Get me out of here!' Today, because you are not saying much, I see you as passive, weak, and effeminate, and I feel that you have abandoned me. So I have become passive and afraid to aggressively display my masculinity. I fear that if I become aggressive, you will criticize me for being hairy and masculine. I now see that I have

---

[1]Loeb's patient, the transsexual little boy, James, who is presented in Chapter 7 of this book, had had no contact with homosexuals, but he understood the psychodynamics of *The Wizard of Oz*. In her paper, Dr. L. Loeb writes, "Then castration themes began to predominate in James's play. He pretended to be Dorothy in *The Wizard of Oz*, who was seeking *shoes* for herself, a *heart* for the Tin Man, a *brain* for the Straw Man, and *courage* for the Cowardly Lion—all symbols of penises."

always gone to male doctors and male psychotherapists to find a powerful father substitute to make me feel safe."[2]

881. "I've done everything I can to get something from you, and I'm frustrated like I was with my parents. I want you to give me permission to get sexually unstuck."

883. Pete says he can display aggression only when a woman-driver's car gets in the way of his car. When this happens, he gets furious, honks, and passes her car as soon as possible.

906. Dream: *"You, I, and a third person are participating in my psychoanalysis."* Association: "The *third person* is my unconscious mind. I would prefer to have you leave me out and talk directly to my unconscious mind."

915. Last visit, I extended his time an extra fifteen minutes. This visit he tells me that if I continue to be "too nice" to him, he fears that he might become "too dependent" on me and, therefore, "vulnerable to rejection."

949. Pete is sullen. I point this out. He says that he feels rejected and furious because a woman patient did not leave my office until two minutes after his session was to have begun. I tell him that, although he has insisted that he is not dependent on me, whenever I have begun one of his sessions more than one minute late, he has felt rejected and become furious. He says that he has to admit that in spite of his vow to "never become dependent on anyone again" he has become dependent on me.

950. Dreams: I. *"A man is about to make love to me, but he turns away and masturbates."* II. *"I'm running to catch a plane, but I forgot my suitcase."* Associations: "The *man turning away to masturbate* represents your beginning our last session two minutes late. My having *forgotten my suitcase* represents my not having the balls to confront you." It is apparent to him that he is transferring onto me the feelings of abandonment he had felt toward his mother when his sister was born and toward his father for "not being there" for him.

952. "Last night I fantasied putting an ad in the paper saying that I was a gay man looking for a woman."

959. Dream: *"I fear that I will be punished for watching a movie that encourages women to have sex with teenagers. A woman comes*

---

[2]Like Dr. L. Loeb's patient, James (see chapter 7), Pete feels that unlike his castrating mother, a powerful male has a penis and does not need to steal his penis.

in through my window to strangle me with a rope." Associations: As an adolescent he feared that his mother would *strangle* or castrate him if he became sexual with her.

963. "I'm confused. I don't seem to want men so much anymore. I fear that I might think of marrying a woman."

971. "I visited my sixty-nine-year-old mother. She was not cold to me. I was cold to her. I'm still angry at her. I kept my distance. She had trouble going down the stairs, but I couldn't force myself to hold her arm to help her. I should have, but I got scared. I feel bad about that. I can't show warmth or affection to her—or anyone. If I could be affectionate with her, could I be affectionate with someone else? When she dies, will I be a mess with guilt for rejecting her. In reality, my parents are not people that I need or ought to fear or hate."

973. Yesterday, when he arrived, my office door was closed. Although he knew that he was supposed to ring my buzzer when he arrived, he did not ring it because he assumed that I was with a woman patient and that I did not want him to disturb us. Eventually he left, and missed his session. I told him that I had been in my office alone waiting for him to buzz. He recognized that he had again acted out his mother-transference with me.

974. Dream: *"I was a lonely, frightened child."* Association: "That's how I felt yesterday when I found your door closed."

980. He says that he keeps having involuntary thoughts of becoming heterosexual and wonders if this "represents an unconscious wish." He fears that if he "comes-out heterosexual," his homosexual friends will reject him. He sees that this is a mother-transference.

984. Whenever Zelda asks him to go somewhere with her, he becomes frightened.

987. Dream: *"A woman tells me that I can't do something, but a man says it's legal."* Association: "The dream is clearly a wish that my father had told me that I could do what I felt my mother had told me not to do."

1002. "Last night I had an orgasm while fantasying that a woman was humping on top of me."

1005. Pete again observes that, although he proclaims that he does not care whether I am silent, late, or away, he becomes furious and gets a stomachache if I am silent, late, or away. During his psychoanalysis, he has repeatedly become aware of this, but then has forgotten this. He again concludes that he needs to deny his love feelings for me because he fears I will reject him for having them.

1008. A woman, with whom he has had a close, platonic friendship for ten-years, suddenly stops returning his phone calls. "When she doesn't call back, I feel like a helpless, rejected, abandoned little boy. I feel lonely, angry, afraid, and immobilized. I pretend that I don't care, but being ignored is such a horrible feeling that, when I don't have to work, I find myself hiding in bed all day. The feeling is similar to how I felt when you were late. In the past I dissipated my loneliness by cruising. Am I most afraid of being abandoned or of my anger at being abandoned?"

1015. "The positive feeling that I am developing toward you is spreading to other people. It's fascinating how uncomfortable that makes me feel."

1032. "When someone puts their penis into my anus, I feel that I'm getting something that I don't have—something that I wanted, but didn't get, from my father. I feel that I'm getting permission to have a penis and use it."

Pete tells me that he had intercourse with women only three times with three different women. All three aggressively initiated sex, and sat on top of him. He doesn't know whether he had orgasms. They were aggressive top-women. Each time, afterwards, he was "compelled to cruise and find a top-man."

1081. Dream: *"A vending machine has many holes in it, and I'm trying to decide which hole to urinate into."* Association: *"I'm trying to decide* whether to put my penis into an anus, a mouth, or a vagina."

1095. Pete hired both a man and a woman to come to his house for sex. He was extremely anxious while waiting for them to arrive. After they came, he was able to relax because they were playful and light-hearted. The woman took off her clothing and masturbated him to orgasm. Emphatically, he said, "The experience didn't change anything."

1112. Dream: *"My father shoots an apple off my head with a bow and arrow."* He Associates to William Tell, who *shot an apple off* his son's head *with an arrow*. The *apple* reminds him of the Garden of Eden. The *arrow* reminds him both of the snake in the Garden of Eden and of his recurrent childhood nightmare of a *snake coming out of the cupboard*. He concludes that the *apple* represented his mother and that the *arrow* represented his father's penis. He believes that the dream means that he had wished that his father had *come out of the cupboard* and had separated him from his mother by shooting her off of his head—i.e., out of his mind.

1113. Pete complains that I have not raised his fee to keep up with inflation. I point out that he wants me to set a limit on him just as he wanted his father to do in the dream he had yesterday. I raise his fee.

1117. Dream: *"I'm a warden in a prison controlling rowdy inmates."* He realizes that this dream also expresses his wish for external limits.

1191. He recounts several incidents in which he tried, unsuccessfully, to provoke his father into setting limits on him.

1194. He notes that he has become "less defensive, freer, and more flippant" with me.

1201. "When you break your silence and talk to me, your words are like baby oil massaged onto me. I'm very uncomfortable with the positive feelings that I have begun to feel toward you."

1203. "I feel there is a latent heterosexual in me that is trying to come out. This reminds me of my childhood nightmare of '*a snake coming out of the cupboard.*'"

1211. "In the analysis, I've become aware that I want more than sex. I feel lonely, and I want a relationship—like the one I might have had with my mother before my sister was born."

1227. Dream: *"A woman rejects me because I have a penis."*

1230. "I'm getting over my fear of having positive feelings for you, but I fear trying it with a real person."

1231. Dream: *"I'm eating in a Spanish restaurant. An old Spanish lady says 'It's spring,' and I say, 'No, it's winter.' She says, 'watch your back,' and a man tries to cut my head off."* Associations: "*The old Spanish lady* is my mother who tells me to return from the winter (the time after my sister's birth) to the *spring* (the time before her birth), but I fear that if I do so, my father will castrate me. You are at my *back*."

1254. Dream: *"I'm at a conference in a forest. I lose control and shit in my pants. It runs down my leg. I get to an outhouse, but it's full of shit. So I track down another outhouse and try to clean myself up—but I get shit all over me. My mother and brother are watching. Zelda walks by, and I duck so she won't see me."* Associations: "I think of anal intercourse. In the third grade at school I *lost control and shit in my pants*. The last session, I talked about being stuck and not being able to love. Then I dream that *'I lose control and shit.'* Do I fear that if I loosen up and let myself love someone like you or Zelda, it would be like losing control, shitting in my pants, and being rejected for it? My mother rejected my shit. She was a cleanliness freak."

1255. Crying, he says, "I was frightened all weekend, and I hid in bed. I'm stuck. I can't let go."

1256. Crying, he says, "I'm stuck, I can't accept my normal feelings because my mother wouldn't accept them."

1257. Dreams: I. *"I'm driving. My parents are in the car.* II. *I pee, but the toilet seat won't stay up, and I pee all over it. My father ignores it."* Associations: "I can't be aggressive and in control when I'm awake, but I can be in my dream." I. "I wish that my father had allowed me to be dominant, take control, and be the driver. II. My father does not object to my standing up and aggressively urinating like a man."

1261. "Last night, before going to bed, I saw some attractive women on TV. I had to keep my sexual energy in check. I don't know whether the sexual energy was heterosexual or homosexual, but it kept me awake most of the night."

1272. "I still can't express my attachment or love feelings I feel toward you because I fear you will reject me. Any thought of my becoming attached is threatening. Right now, I feel like provoking an argument with you. I feel like attacking you before you attack me. I know that this is mother transference."

1275. "Having a man initiate sex has always been safe, I fear that if I were to initiate body contact with you, you would reject me."

1279. Dream: "*I was giving dancing lessons to Mexican girls. I was enjoying the dancing, not the girls. A Spanish mobster came to get me. I was afraid and tried to placate him.*" Associations: "In high school I was a good dancer and danced with many *Mexican girls*. They were friends, not girlfriends. For me it was asexual. The *Spanish mobster*, my father, *came to get me* for *dancing* with the *Mexican girls*, my mother. Did I become a passive homosexual partner to placate men, who represented my father, so they wouldn't *come to get me?*"

1283. "For the first time in my life, I was able to masturbate to orgasm fantasying that I was a top-man. In the fantasy, you were a top-man who wanted to screw me, but I fought you off."

1291. Pete has a slip of the tongue and says that his sister is dead when he meant to say something else. This convinces him that when his sister was born, he had wished her dead. He then retrieves a memory, that had been repressed, of his having left his three-year-old sister in the middle of a busy street.

1292. Dream: "I was getting married to a woman that I didn't know. She looked like a lesbian I saw at a gay bar. She was wearing a man's tuxedo. I simultaneously felt 'she is very attractive' and 'get me out of here.' Many things prevented the marriage."

1293. "I fear becoming dependent upon a woman even more than I fear becoming dependent on a man."

1294. "More and more, I hate being alone. If the loneliness I now feel is what I felt as a child, it must have been horrible."

1295. Dream: *"I couldn't find my briefcase or my calendar.* I have not had one of those castration dreams for a while."

1301. "I dreamed that 'I was *remodeling my house.'*" Association: Part of me wants to change.

1306. Dream: *"I'm in front of a group of people. I have nothing on but my underwear. I cover myself with a pad of paper and promise to wear clothing the next time."* Association: "I'm more open and less afraid of being exposed."

[During sessions 1317 to 1376 he worked on his father-transference feelings toward me, and his mother transference toward my wife (whose office is next to mine).]

1317. Dream: *"I go into your wife's office and lay down on her couch facing her."* Association: "Your wife must represent my mother. Maybe I should be in analysis with her."

1331. Dreams: I. *"I was in bed, and a large black object was coming toward me"* I awoke in terror, yelling, "Get away!" II. *"My mother was throwing my clothing and belongings out on the street."* Associations: I. "The *large black object* was you, your wife, and my mother coming to cut off my penis." II. "*My mother* represented you, your wife, and my mother rejecting me by *throwing my clothing and things out on the street.* . . . I don't want to move in with you and have dinner. Maybe I should go into Loretta's office."

1354. "When you put a positive spin on things, instead of feeling supported, I take it negatively. I'm afraid to see you as a loving, supportive, parent-figure because I fear you will reject me for wanting it, like my mother did."

1355. "I fantasied being a top-man with a passive man. It scared me. That could lead me to be sexually aggressive with women. Although part of me wants to feel love for you and be intimate with you, I battle against it. I don't want to give up this defense."

1356. "I'm turning you into my mother, instead of making you into a father figure to identify with."

1363. "I don't like being alone, but I don't want to admit that I want to hook up with someone."

1365. Dream: *"I was flying in a huge plane. It was dangerously tilting and shaking in a storm. I was frightened. A week later, I was in the same plane again, and it was going to happen again. This time I was in the cockpit, but I wanted to be in the cabin. We took off. I knew that, although it would be scary, nothing bad would happen."* Associations: "The moral of the story is: My *flying in a huge plane* that *was dangerously tilting and shaking in a storm* represented the dangerously tilting and shaking relationship I had with my mother when I was a small boy. Then, although *I was frightened*, I survived. The dream meant that if it were to *happen again* with some other woman, *although it would be scary, nothing bad would happen,* and I would again survive. Also, with some other woman, I would not have to be *in the cabin*—passive and vulnerable, I could be in the cockpit—active and in control."

1369. Dreams: I. *"I'm attracted to a series of women."* II. *"I'm being chased."* III. *"I'm in a car. Three men are trying to break into it. I woke up kicking and screaming, 'Police!'"* Associations: "I. If I'm *attracted to women,* II. *men* will *chase me,* III. *break* in, and castrate me. I want a strong *police*man to protect me."

1370. "Yesterday, I felt sexually attracted to a woman the way I felt toward the *series of women* in yesterday's dream. She was pregnant and came across as a warm, loving mother. I felt like a little kid attracted to a good mother. It was a bizarre and unique experience. Was I attracted to my mother when she was pregnant with my sister? Telling you this makes me feel closer to you, but frightens me. Do I fear that you, representing my father, will become angry and castrate me for being sexually attracted to the woman, who represented my mother? In my past dreams I feared my mother would castrate me. In yesterday's dream I feared men would. Today, although I know that my finding the woman attractive doesn't displease you, I fear that you will castrate me for it. Is my passive seduction of men a way to please them so that they won't castrate me?"

1376. "I want you to be a strong, married, heterosexual father figure who will coach me to become straight. That is what I seek when I cruise. However, on the other hand, I also fear that if I do become straight, you will become angry and dangerous. I feel that you will accept me only if I remain passive sexually. My mother, not my father, sent messages that I should not be masculine. Why was I afraid of my father? That's Oedipal, and I'm amazed! As a boy I felt that if I hid my penis, neither parent would become angry. I felt that the only way I could have a good relationship with my parents was to pretend that I didn't have a penis. I had an unusual relationship with my mother. Because she was so frustrating and frightening, I identified with her and clandestinely colluded with her in a platonic alliance against my father. I have always wanted a man—now you—to show me how to be masculine, but at the same time I feel that you will become angry and castrating if I do become masculine."

I remind him that it was after he became aware of his having positive feelings for me [in about session 1317] that he developed positive feelings for my wife and had the oedipal dream in which he feared his father.

1378–1380. "When I come five days a week, the psychoanalysis becomes more intense. It's like living with someone. Now I need more than just getting off with someone. I also need a relationship. . . . Because I was not a girl, my mother rejected me and my masculinity. So I moved into the basement. I was not afraid of being alone in the basement [separation anxiety]. Although in my childhood, as far as I'm aware, no one ever threatened me with castration, I have always been terrified that, if my masculinity showed, I would be castrated [castration anxiety]. The only way I could get an erection and achieve an orgasm was to submit sexually, either in fantasy or in reality, to a powerful, masculine, father figure. Whenever I try to masturbate while fantasying that I'm with a woman, I lose my erection. I now know that I lose my erection because unconsciously, I fear castration. Whenever either a man or a woman has wanted me to become an aggressive sexual partner, I have become frightened, impotent, and angry. Had I not been frightened, I would not have been impotent and angry. If you had told me that my problem was oedipal, I wouldn't have believed you, but now it has become obvious. I still have the ridiculous, preposterous feeling that if I display any sexual interest in women, especially in your wife, you will become angry. I now see that my mother was being seductive when she colluded with me against my father, and that I feared he would castrate me for it. It's been relatively easy for me to recognize that my mother rejected my masculinity. However, it's been difficult for me to recognize that I feared that my father would castrate me if I became too close to my mother." [He has here become aware of his oedipal guilt and fear of castration.]

1381. "Today, I fantasied that I was back in school, and I castrated a boy for peeing on a toilet seat. I've never had a fantasy like that before."

1413. "I see women's genitals as wounds, and I get turned off by them."

1414. Dream I: "*I was in the cockpit of a plane. It was trying to take off, from an underground building. It was taxiing, with wings folded, through small doors. The plane got outside, but I had to disembark because something was wrong with it. I walked around, but could not find the right gate. I lost my luggage, and I panicked that I would miss my flight.*" II: "*I was working under the covers in a bed with a woman-colleague-competitor. She explained that I needed insurance, but then she decided that I didn't need it.*" Associations: "The plane was a penis. It had to get smaller to get through a small opening. Last night I watched a porno movie showing female genitalia. It didn't turn me on. Like in my other dreams, losing my luggage meant castration."

1415. He says that he wants me to love him as a whole person, that is, as a person with a penis.

1419. "Both my fear of rejection and my fear of castration make me inhibit my sexual impulses. Then I become angry, and I have to inhibit my anger."

1422. Dream: "*I was embarrassed because my baldness was showing.*" Association: "I fear that people will see that my penis is too small."

1432. "You look different today, happier. Normally, I avoid looking at you. I'm afraid to tell anyone that I'm attracted to them and feel love for them. Today, I feel it here, but I'm afraid to talk about it. It would be safe because no sex and no sexual rejection will happen here."

1433. Dream: "*A man came into my bedroom to harm, castrate, or kill me. He was white-haired and wore glasses.* I awoke terrified and couldn't go back to sleep." Associations: "I felt glad to be with you yesterday. Then I dreamed that *someone with white hair and glasses*—that is you—would *kill or castrate me.* When I became glad to be with my first analyst, he told me that I couldn't go any further and ended my psychoanalysis." [I suspected that Pete's first psychoanalyst aborted the psychoanalysis and rejected Pete because the first psychoanalyst became afraid of his own homosexual countertransference feelings toward Pete.]

I remind him that when he began to worry that he might be in love with Don, he had awakened with similar fears of castration, harm, or death. I also point out to him that recently when our sessions are over, he has begun to look at me, smile, and say goodbye, instead of just running out of my office as he often did in the past.

1444. "I feel bad that you are about to leave on vacation. I have not allowed myself to feel that way before."

1510. Pete says that I am the first psychotherapist that has not urged him to become heterosexual. He then tells me that he has a new female friend, Gil. She is a psychoanalytically oriented psychotherapist. They go to movies together. She is several years younger than he, is widowed, and is looking for a new husband. She knows that he is homosexual and so does not regard him as a potential husband. "Last night, while masturbating, I tried to fantasy that I was fucking Gil. It didn't work. I finally got off by fantasying that some man was eating his girlfriend's pussy."

1514. "I'm terrified that if I made a pass at Gil, she would reject me." He again notes that he has never had both affectionate and sexual feelings for the same person. He has had sexual feelings for some men and affectionate feelings for some women.

1519. "I'm losing my strong desire to find a man who will give me what I don't have. Sex with men has become boring. However, I don't know how to feel turned on by a woman. I feel dependent on you, but I fear being dependant on a woman."

1522. "It made me incredibly uncomfortable when you told me that most women want men to be sexually aggressive with them. I can't deal with the thought of loving, nurturing, and protecting a woman. The thought makes me want to cruise. I feel that if I had sex with a woman, it would be an abusive rape. This goes back to my anger at my mother when she rejected my masculine aggressiveness."

1530. "I told Gil that, recently in my psychoanalysis, I have become confused about my sexual orientation. Telling her that made me feel exposed and vulnerable, but she didn't reject me—not yet."

1533. Dream: *"I'm with a woman in a bakery, and I lost something. The bakery only had food that neither of us could eat."* Associations: "I think of forbidden fruit—sex. Gil is attractive. That frightens me and makes me want to cruise to find men for protection." He says that he has not had sex with a man for several months.

1543. "When I see a naked woman in a film, I get angry. I think, 'You can't seduce me. You can't make me do it.'"

1552–1568. Although, he consciously knows that I would not object, or become angry with him, if he were to become masculinely sexually aggressive, he nevertheless feels that I would become angry, and he becomes terrified. He realizes that this is because his mother wished him to be a girl and rejected his masculinity.

1584. Dream: *"Gil intended to say, 'Do you want to come to my house?' but she had a slip of the tongue and said 'Do you want to come to my bed.' She became embarrassed and walked away."* Associations: "You think that the dream means that I want to go to bed with her, but that I can't admit it consciously. I have that thought too, but I don't believe it. I wish Gil would become sexually aggressive with me—like a top-man. I was able to have the dream-wish because you gave me an extra 15 minutes yesterday, and I felt you cared about me."

[He then resumes working through his oedipal transference that he began working on during sessions 1317 through 1376.]

1588. Dream: "*I was in your wife's office with her and two or three other men. Because I was the tallest, I attempted to remove a burned-out light bulb and screw in a new one. I failed to screw in the new one and the entire fixture came down. Someone said that I didn't know how to do it and that he would screw it in.*" Association: "In the dream I *failed* in my attempt to *screw* (for) your *wife.*"

1594. "Last night I tried to masturbate while fantasying a woman, but I became frightened and lost my erection."

1611. "I watched a straight film in which there was passionate, aggressive, lovemaking—just what I fear. However, the woman laughed with pleasure while having intercourse. Gay films show fucking, not lovemaking. I want someone to passionately love me sexually so that I can be released and have an orgasm. I had hoped to get that from you, but I project onto you the rejection of my masculinity, which I got from my mother."

1621. "My affection for you frightens me, and I can't talk about it. Being angry with you is much easier. That's sick, isn't it?"

1622. "I am experiencing, toward you, the love that I couldn't feel toward my mother. She never said, 'I love you,' Instead she repeatedly said, that I was a 'rotten miserable brat.' It's foreign to me to exchange love feelings with anyone. I couldn't do it with my mother. I wonder if my straight siblings could do it with my mother?"

1629. "In here, my fear of both rejection and castration feels so real, but it isn't."

1635. "To have positive, love feelings for you, or for anyone, is abnormal for me. I habitually defend against such feelings. Now, I hate to be alone. However, I don't know whether I can change, because I'm more curious about men's bodies than I am women's bodies."

1637. "In the transference I still get angry at you both for being a rejecting mother and for not being a protecting, top-man, father."

1639. "I feel blocked from having sex with a woman the same way I'm blocked from telephoning my mother."

1640. Dream: *"A woman got into bed with me and started playing around with me. It woke me up, but I was not afraid."*

1650. "I had a sexual fantasy about you for the first time. Boy, this is uncomfortable. There is no reason for my feeling uncomfortable. Is my feeling comfortable, while fantasying playing around with you sexually, putting sex and love together? I did it this morning. I already know, but tell me, that it's not unusual for patients to have sexual fantasies about playing around sexually with their analysts. Today, I came in here wearing a T-shirt and fantasied that it might seduce you. Is it progress for me to put both friendship and sex together?" I respond that just because he believed that his mother was offended by his masculinity and his sexual aggressiveness, does not mean that I too am offended.

1654. "I became upset and lonely when Gil said she was busy and could not go to a movie with me. I don't like being alone. Cruising for sex or getting a massage doesn't help much anymore. This weekend I wondered if I would feel free and good and if I could aggressively enter someone and not be a hung-up, frightened child."

1658. "I saw a film about bisexuals. Afterwards, I successfully masturbated while fantasying that I was sucking on a woman's breast. Then I became furious—enraged. I thought 'I won't do that.' . . . I *feel* you're gonna be angry if I like women yet I *know* that's not true."

1659. "I woke up this morning thinking how lucky I am, to be coming here to talk with you. I have always avoided feeling that way. I'm frustrated that I don't get what I want from you. Is it mother or father transference that I can't ask you for what I want?"

1661. He says, "When I came in today, you were friendly and said hello, but I couldn't reciprocate. I can't be friendly with you, or my parents, or anyone else. I fear emotional intimacy."

I again tell Pete that he is separating his sexual feelings for me from his affectionate feelings for me. I remind him that this pattern began when his mother simultaneously encouraged him to have an affectionate, platonic relationship with her, while calling him a "rotten miserable brat" if he displayed any masculine aggressiveness. I also remind him that he has done to others what his mother did to him. He did it to Don, Gil, and many others. He replies, "I can't put into words the feelings that I'm reliving from my childhood. I'm being back into re-experiencing a situation that was horrible."

1673. I summarize for Pete and tell him that with Don, who was a bottom man, he became his mother and did to Don what his mother had done to him. However, with top men he becomes the mother he wished he had, and he encourages them to be aggressive toward him the way he wished his mother had encouraged him to be aggressive toward her. He realizes that this is true.

1688. "I hate being alone, but I'm afraid to get involved. I think of looking for a woman, but I'm turned on by men."

1716. "To relieve my back pains, I need to lose weight again. This time, however, instead of joining a gay gym, I joined a straight one. My trainer is a small, non-homosexual, man—a cute little sweetheart. While masturbating, I fantasied that I was going to fuck him, but when I was about to enter him, I lost my erection. I felt that I was not allowed to do it. I feel you will emasculate me for even talking about this. Where in my childhood could that have come from? In childhood, a person doesn't think of entering anyone. The prohibition against my entering anyone is so real, and my need to inhibit my entering someone is so strong, I don't see how I can get over it."

1727. Dream: *"Your wife was there. A hand comes toward my leg. I kick it away and yell, 'No! No! Get away!' I run to my car to flee, but the street is blocked."*

1728. "I'm enormously frustrated sexually. I can't have a heterosexual fantasy—even in a dream. I get turned on to men, not to women." I point out that he is assuring me that I don't need to worry about the sexual thoughts he had about my wife in his last dream because he is too afraid to do anything sexual with a woman.

1730. Dream: *"I bought a duplex and was living on one side. I rented the other side to a straight* [non-homosexual] *Asian man. He was screaming orders to another guy who did what he was told."* Associations: "When I was about five or six, I repeatedly fantasied that I had an *Asian* twin on the *opposite side* of the world. The *straight Asian man* in the dream must have been my *Asian* twin who was being a dominant top-man to the other *guy who did what he was told.* That could have been a wish to be straight."

Dream: *"I was having sex with my older brother. He was the top-man. I was very uncomfortable."* Associations: "I never before even had the thought of having sex with my brother. I don't think it ever happened. I shared a room with my brother comfortably for four years. However, when I then went into puberty and I began to have wet dreams, I became curious about his penis, and I became uncomfortable when I saw him in his underwear. So I insisted on moving into my sister's room, and she moved in with my brother. I haven't thought about that for years. Could I have desired him sexually?"

"I'm so horny, lonely, and frightened that, when I don't have to work, I can't get out of bed. Now I seem to want more than sex. I also want a relationship."

1732. Dream: *"I'm next to a toilet in a bathroom. I'm trying to pee through a hole in the top of an empty Kleenex box. A big, muscular man comes in and we engage in a very clever, funny dialogue. He isn't my brother, but I think he is. Seductively, he says that we have to be quiet. I then become afraid to pee in the Kleenex box, and we go across the hall into my sister's bedroom."* I woke up sexually frustrated that I can't get sexual satisfaction and that I'm lonely. Association: "Yesterday, there was an empty Kleenex box in the Gym, and I wondered how they get Kleenex to pop up. The box's opening reminded me of a vagina. I'm confused about vaginal openings. I have no interest in naked women's breasts. My sexual fantasy when I masturbate is not about having sex. It's about the clothes and the appearance of a big powerful man."

1733. "My self-image is that I'm not a man, nor is it that I'm a woman. When I get a man off, I feel he won't be angry with me if I get off, so I can get-off. I don't like being alone."

1747. I was five minutes late to our session, so Pete came downstairs to get me. He said, "I could not have done that two months ago, because that would be like being a top-man. It infuriates me to play the top-man role. I avoid it."

1749. "Being afraid and stuck is no fun. I don't know what to do. When I don't have to work, I go to bed and hide. . . . I didn't get what I needed when I was a child, and I'm furious. I want to be a bottom-man so I can get what I need. I don't want to be a top-man and give. I had to take care of myself so early. I want you to give to me by talking to me. Let someone do for me." I tell him that he is furious for not "getting" enough when he was a child, and that now, because he fears this anger, he will not let himself become aggressive and get what he wants.

1758. Dream: *"I was driving and confused about where I was going. I couldn't get there."* Associations: "Having positive feelings for you, frightens me. Yesterday, you were talkative and helpful so I had positive feelings for you, but I felt threatened by those feelings. It's becoming clear that I get frightened whenever I have love feelings for anyone."

1762. Dream: *"I was trying to squeeze something out of a container, but instead of coming out the opening, it came out in three or four other places. It was a mess."* Associations: "Last night, while cruising on the internet, two bisexual men ejaculated while fantasying that they were eating another man's ejaculate out of a woman's vagina. To me, that was both disgusting and frightening. Oh! That is the meaning of the dream! To me, female genitalia are a mess of holes. I wish I could get over my disgust with, and fear of, female genitalia. When I was ten or eleven I took one of mother's tampons and tried to figure out where to put it inside me. I was confused. Did I think I was a woman? I'm still confused about who and what I am. It's so hard to get over the disgust, fear, and inhibition. That's the bottom line—the disgust, the fear of castration, and the inhibition."

1763. "When I think of vaginas, I get frightened and feel 'get me out of here.' It's now clear that I fear female genitalia because I feel that they are the result of castration. As far as I'm concerned, women don't have genitals. I'm very frightened of castration. When I think of castration, I get physical pain in my stomach. All of this is confusing. When I try to think of having sex with a woman, I can't picture having sex with a woman. I keep both seeing you as accepting me as a man, and as a potential castrator. My gut reaction is, 'Get me out of here!'"

1764. "If I stopped coming here, I would need some other affectionate, nonsexual relationship with a male therapist for support. [This is the first time that Pete told me this.] Ever since I was 18, I've been in treatment with one or another male psychotherapist. By going to them, I was able to overcome my *anxiety* and *loneliness*. By cruising for one-night-stands with top-men, I was able to overcome my *horniness*. I never thought of that before. I came here because I was *anxious*. If I stopped coming here, I would become *anxious* again."[3]

---

[3] In session 854. Pete told me that gay men idealize Judy Garland. When gay men say, "Let's go find Dorothy," gay men mean "Let's go find homosexual sex." We psychoanalyze this and conclude that homosexual men revere Judy Garland because she helped the three incomplete males in *The Wizard of Oz* replace their missing parts: She helped the Straw Man seek a brain, the Tin Man seek a heart, and the Lion seek courage. Thus, she is the antithesis of Pete's mother, who seemed to object to his masculine attributes. Like Pete, these three flawed males "cruised" the yellow brick road to find an idealized, powerful, Big-Daddy-Wizard who would give them their missing masculine parts. However, when they found the Wizard, he turned out to be a pretentious, powerless, phony who told them that they already had the masculine parts (the penis) that they thought that they lacked. Pete now recognized that he sought male-psychotherapist-Big-Daddy-Wizards to gain his missing masculinity.

1765. "All my relationships with psychotherapists have been platonic, not sexual. I now see that this is what you meant when you told me that I separate my platonic relationships from my sexual ones. When I began to have both sets of feelings toward my only other psychoanalyst, he never psychoanalyzed it. He told me that I could go no further in my psychoanalysis. I fear losing you and being alone. I fear having sexual feelings for you, which I don't see as a solution. I've recreated the same model [transference] with you that I've had with all my former psychotherapists. Would it be a sign of progress if I suddenly allowed myself to have both affectionate and sexual feelings for you?"

1770. He again says that when I am silent, he sees me in the transference as his passive father and he becomes anxious. On the other hand, when I talk, he sees me as an aggressive top-man and his anxiety is alleviated.

1782. He watched movies showing clitorises before and after clitoral circumcision. He became disgusted and too afraid to look. He says that he has been afraid to look, ever since he was a child. He says he "knows that is nutty." He feels that his penis is too small and that he has to get one from a top-man.

1787. He finds himself getting angry and aggressive with friends. He says that he has never done that before.

1790. We are separating for vacations, and he again feels bad about it. He had not remembered that he had felt the same way the last time we both went on vacation.

1798. "I feel that you will oppose my becoming either aggressive or sexual, so I inhibit myself and get the urge to cruise for gay sex, which to me is safe. You turn into my nonaccepting, rejecting, frustrating, rigid, mother. It is mother transference. I'm conscious of it here. I do it with women unconsciously. They are real feelings, but when I talk about them, they are nonsensical. I'm doing it to myself, but I feel like it's an external danger. I know that you don't object to my having sex with women. In fact I think that you represent the heterosexual society." [He laughs.]

1800. He is silent for 30 minutes and then says that he cannot talk to me because he feels connected to me. He fears that if he connects he will be frustrated or castrated.

1811. He realizes that he has been going to male psychiatrists for years to try to get the masculinity he lacks.

1813. Dream: *"I was angry because someone had taken away my king-sized bed and given me a twin-sized bed, and that made me have to sleep alone."*

1821. "Last time, I felt you were more real and less transference, and I became frightened and inhibited. As a child I wished to have a father that loved me and that I could identify with as a male. That wish was coupled with, and negated by, castration anxiety—which left me nowhere."

1825. He says he is terrified of becoming "freed-up."

1828. Dream: *"My brother lost my car and I couldn't find it."* Associations: "My brand-new car represents my penis. My brother, who is three years older than I, threw me against a wall because I was fighting with his friend. My head got cut, and I needed three stitches. Later he hit me with a barrel and knocked out two of my front teeth. Both wounds represented castration to me." He tells me that this was the main reason he had insisted on moving out of the room he shared with his brother, not just because he had sexual feelings for his brother.

1830. Dream: *"I lost my hairpiece and put on a cap so that people wouldn't see my baldness."* Association: "Again, that represents my fear of castration."

1838. "I phoned my father, and was able to talk to him for the first time. I invited him to take a trip to where he was born in Mexico. He readily accepted. It's now very clear to me that when I cruise, I am looking for the father figure that I didn't have."

1840. This hour, while crying, he tells me that he can't trust that anyone will be there for him. He expects criticism, and says that he now understands what I have meant by his fearing abandonment. He says he has regressed back to feeling the emotions and affects that he had not wanted to remember. He now understands that he had had to choose between his mother and his penis. "I spent a lifetime hiding and denying what I am, a man."

1845. He has suddenly remembered a formerly repressed, unconscious memory from his fifth year. He clearly recalls that he frequently "played doctor" with, and closely examined the genitals of the seven-year-old little girl who lived next door. He is amazed to realize that, at that time, he had had heterosexual interest in, and curiosity about, the girl's genitals. He also remembers that they had abruptly stopped playing together. He could not remember why they stopped, but speculated that they must have been caught and that he had been "dreadfully reprimanded and severely punished by his mother."

1850. "I feel freed up and less afraid, and feel that I no longer have to hide my penis. . . . I feel like a little boy who wants to go out and play with little boys. It is like a complete regression to my childhood and my starting over. It's like I'm freed up, and I don't have to hide my penis. I can now masturbate thinking of women, but it is still hard. I am a man! Free! I can wear, and am wearing, boxer shorts—but it is difficult. I don't have to be female."

1853. He tells me that his transference toward me has changed: He is trusting of me and is able to relax on the couch and is not worrying that I might see his penis.

1860. "For the first time, I actually wanted to have intercourse with a woman. I felt it was ridiculous to have a penis and not fuck a woman. Very strange! I don't have thoughts like that. I did not deny the sexual feelings that I never had before. It all began when I saw a play in which there was nudity and no inhibition. The simulated fucking started it all. No one was afraid. It seemed so easy. I don't have to hide. I want to be free." I tell him that he wants to have a male identification now—like he had wanted to have a male identification when he put on his father's boxer shorts.

1870. He is now searching on the internet for a woman to have sex with and possibly a relationship.

1873. He went to a straight bar and talked to a drunk woman. She told him she was 'Humpty Dumpty, Hump, Hump, Hump.' He went home and masturbated. While thinking of having sex with her, he ejaculated. He said that this was the first time he could ejaculate while thinking of a woman.

1890. He asked a woman out and took her to dinner and a movie. He was not interested in an ongoing relationship with her because he learned that she had a teenage son.

1895. He had set a date to meet a woman for coffee. Crying, he said that he could not trust anyone, expected criticism, and was not comfortable when he met with her. That day he hid in bed, cried, and denied that he was a man. He says that he now understands that, when he was a small child, he had to choose between being masculine and having his mother like him.

1897. He feels freed-up. He doesn't have to hide his penis and can wear boxer shorts.

PSYCHODYNAMIC FORMULATION

This case shows how, through a psychoanalysis, Pete gradually became aware of, and alleviated, the terrifying childhood experiences that caused both his homosexuality and his transference reactions to his analyst.

During his psychoanalysis, Pete became aware that he often tried to provoke me or start arguments with me either: (1) When, in the transference, he experienced me as his mother. This was because when he was a child, his mother had consistently rejected his masculinity, his penis, and his attempts to aggressively obtain either oral, anal, or genital sexual satisfaction; *or:* (2) When, in the transference, he experienced me as his father. This was because, when he was a child, his father had been relatively absent from him both physically and psychologically and consequently had set few limits on him. Once he became aware of, and understood these transferences, he remembered that, in the past, he had frequently acted out these same transferences with others.

During his psychoanalysis it also became clear to Pete that his early experiences of both separation anxiety and castration anxiety had interfered with his heterosexual development and had led him to develop his homosexual orientation.

The following early experiences led Pete to develop the intense separation anxiety which helped determine his homosexual orientation:

(1) Pete's mother told him that she was very disappointed that he was a boy and that she got pregnant again because she wanted a girl. (2) When Pete was three, his sister was born, and his mother withdrew her attention from him and lavished it on his sister. He felt abandoned, lonely, and destitute. In his desperation he began to suck his thumb, but his mother strongly objected and put pepper on it. He next attempted to regain his mother's love and attention by doing naughty things such as wetting his bed, but she responded with reprimands and further rejection. Then, because his mother often belittled his father, Pete tried to please her by siding with her against his father and by being as *unlike* his father as he could. He went so far as to pretend that he was not a male and that he did not have a penis.

Because Pete felt that his mother consistently rejected all of his masculine, aggressive behavior, and all of his attempts to please her, he eventually withdrew from her, and unconsciously both identified with her as an aggressor (Freud, A. 1946) and incorporated her as a lost love object (Freud, S. 1915). A consequence of this identification and incorporation was that Pete assumed his mother's negative attitudes toward both his own and his father's masculinity. Pete said, "By identifying with my mother's feminine role, I almost left reality and believed that I was a girl."

All this occurred before Pete was five-years-old. Then, at about the age of five, in hopeless despair, Pete turned to his father for solace and support, but his father worked long hours and was unavailable. Eventually, Pete gave up trying to gain either love, approval, or support from either parent, and he vowed "never again" to allow himself to "become dependant on anyone for anything."

The following early experiences led Pete to develop the intense separation anxiety which helped determine his homosexual orientation:

(1) His mother told him that she wished that he had been a girl and then showed preference for his sister.

(2) When Pete stood up to urinate into the toilet—like a man—his mother objected and insisted that he sit down on the toilet and push his penis down between his legs to urinate—like a girl.

(3) When he was 2½-years-old, a woman at the beach tried to help him remove his bathing suit, and he apprehensively had yelled, "No! No! That's mine!" His mother had felt that this was funny and always liked to tell her friends about it.

(4) His mother refused to allow him to become a Cub Scout and told him that "all he wanted was *the uniform*." To him, *the uniform* was a symbolic representation of his masculine identity.

(5) His mother discouraged him from playing aggressive games with boys because they were too "rough."

(6) He only played with girls—not with boys, and his mother thought this was normal.

(7) When Pete displayed any behavior that was aggressive, his mother called him a "rotten miserable brat."

As a child, because his mother actively discouraged Pete's masculine behavior, he became terrified that if he displayed any assertive, aggressive, or masculine behavior, his mother would become displeased and he might have his penis removed. Therefore, Pete inhibited, suppressed, and/or repressed, all of his assertive, aggressive, masculine impulses, fantasies, and actions.

Then, during and following puberty, Pete's separation anxiety and castration anxiety manifested itself as follows:

(1) He distanced himself from his mother by starting arguments with her.

(2) Because by now he had transferred his rejecting, castrating mental image of his mother onto all women, he felt that if he exhibited any erotic or hostile aggression toward them, they too would reject him for being masculine.

(3) The thought of anyone who lacked a penis, both reminded Pete of his mother and terrified him of the possibility of his being castrated. Having sex with such a person turned him off sexually. So he displaced his genital sexual desires away from women and onto "aggressive," "beefy," "older" men. When he was 16, Pete began to "cruise" and seduce powerful-looking, older men. Helping such men ejaculate, enabled him to ejaculate. While doing this, he fantasied that he was a passive, helpless, effeminate person seducing, placating, and sexually gratifying a father figure. He either did this with such a man or masturbated while fantasying that he was doing this with such a man. Through this behavior, he both appeased a father or brother surrogate and avoided having his masculinity spurned by a mother surrogate.

Through his psychoanalysis, Pete recognized that he had had friendship without sex with many women, and sex without friendship with many men. As he said, he "separated sex from friendship and cruised penises, not persons." He was most attracted to men who were married. Through his psychoanalysis, he became consciously aware that this was because, "They were able to have sex with women, and still retain their penises." He said that he always envied men who could be aggressive, and felt that by submitting to such men sexually, he might be able to gain their strength. Pete put it this way, "When someone puts their penis into my anus, I feel that I'm getting something that I don't have, something that I didn't get from my father. Then I get the feeling that its okay to reveal that I have a penis, that is, to let my *snake come out of the cupboard*. Then I can ejaculate."

Pete had never been able to act out the aggressive, top-man role because, unconsciously, he felt that playing that role would be equivalent to (1) his "beating up" the other person, (2) his becoming what his mother had called a "rotten, miserable brat," and (3) his becoming at risk of becoming rejected [separation anxiety] and/or castrated. He eventually understood that he passively seduced and presented his anus to father-figures to please and placate them so that they would both love him and not castrate him. He recognized that both his fear of rejection and his fear of castration caused him to inhibit his sexual impulses.

When Pete was 18, a girl aggressively seduced him, got on top of him, and sat on his erect penis. [He was able to get aroused by a woman.] Although he could not remember exactly what happened after that, he does remember that immediately afterward he felt compelled to cruise and find a top-man who would penetrate his anus. During the latter part of his psychoanalysis, Pete realized that he had had to repress what had happened with the girl for two reasons: (1) Women's genitals turned him off because they frightened him, disgusted him, made him sick to his stomach, and because he saw them as wounds that were the result of castration, and (2) Because his mother had objected to his masculine aggressiveness, he felt that if he had ejaculated with this girl, it would have been an "unacceptable, abusive rape." Thus, through his psychoanalysis, Pete realized that during his early childhood he had unconsciously come to believe that he either had to give up his relationship with his mother or give up his masculinity.

REFERENCES

FREUD, A. (1946). The Ego and the Mechanisms of Defense. *Standard Edition* 19.

FREUD, S. (1915). Mourning and Melancholia. *Standard Edition* 14.

THE PSYCHOANALYSIS OF A PATIENT WITH A FOOT FETISH

CASE PRESENTATION

Bill's parents called Dr. Loretta Loeb and told her that they were worried that their forty-five-year-old son might commit suicide. They told her that, beginning in his childhood, he had often been depressed, and that, as an adult, he had always had difficulty earning a living or forming a lasting relationship with a woman.

Initial Evaluation

When Dr. L. Loeb telephoned Bill to set up an appointment, he said that his parents had not cared that he had not been home in many years. After he had told them that he was depressed, they began calling him daily. After he told his parents of his depression, his father sarcastically said that he would "buy him an analyst." I began seeing Bill six days a week because of his concern that he might be suicidal.

Bill looked like a derelict when he came to our first session. His hair was unkempt, and his fingernails were chewed. His clothing was disheveled, ill-fitting, and dirty. He used a great deal of reaction formation with me by subserviently asking me what he should do and repeatedly saying "yes ma'am." Bill told me that his present unhappiness began two years ago when his second marriage ended. However, he recently became "extremely despondent, anxious, and depressed" when his twenty-year-old girlfriend, Doris, told him that he had been "too aggressive with her" and left him. After she left, he felt that he "had nothing to live for," and he "could not eat, sleep, or stop crying." He said that he had been able to do anything he wanted to do with her. For example, he had put vegetables and his whole hand into her vagina, and he had "butt-fucked" her. He had called her degrading names and, at times, he had refused to talk or eat with her. Bill stressed, however, that he had never abused her physically. Every time he mentioned Doris, he promptly changed the subject, spoke about his mother, and cried. He said that he had always gone with "down and out, disorganized, and low status women like Doris." This included each of his two previous wives. Even though he bought these women nice things, eventually they left him. With all these women he had frequent premature ejaculations and was occasionally impotent.

When he was six, Bill had been sent to his first psychoanalyst because he was sad and his parents did not like his behavior. In his twenties, he saw a second psychoanalyst for three years because he had not been able to establish a stable relationship with any woman. Recently, he had been in psychotherapy with a transactional analyst.

Bill described his seventy-year-old father as "intelligent, domineering, self-righteous, distant, and lonely." His father had inherited a fortune, which he had increased substantially. Bill had grown up on a secluded "gentleman's farm" because his father "did not like being around people." Therefore, when growing up, Bill had no playmates. He vividly remembered that, when he was eight, his father had become jealous of certain letters that his mother had received, and he had yelled at her while chasing her around the house. Whenever Bill attempted to please his father by succeeding at some task, his father would say, "Anybody could have done that." Bill felt that the only thing that his father ever did for him was to give him money.

Bill described his mother as a "petite, attractive, educated, seductive, brunette." Her interests encompassed fine furnishings, art, and parties. No matter what Bill accomplished, she told him that he could have done better. He had one sibling, a sister, who was three years younger than himself. When Bill was growing up, his parents were only home for meals and to sleep.

Bill's parents had rarely disciplined or set limits on his behavior. For example, when he was four, his parents only laughed, when he urinated on a house plant, and when he used his fingers to serve them cake. They did not stop him from picking his nose or placing the snot on the wall. When he was twelve, his parents said nothing when he smeared their bedroom wall with crayons. Between the ages of sixteen and twenty-one, he ignored his parents' half-hearted objections when he purchased three automobiles and drove around the farm. After Bill had nine auto accidents and could no longer get auto insurance, Bill's father threatened to stop Bill's allowance, but did not. Bill was spanked only twice, both times by his father. Once, when he was six, for ruining his mother's flower garden, and once, when he was eight, for carrying his father's shotgun into the surrounding woods. He was now unhappy that he always "got away with things," and told me that he now always carried a concealed gun. I insisted that he bring me proof of his having gotten rid of the gun, before I would go on with the evaluation. A receipt from a gun dealer for the sale of the gun, and his word that he had no other guns [he had told me that he always told the truth] allowed us to proceed with the evaluation.

In college, Bill played instead of studying. He became involved with his first "down and out" girl whom he had met in a bar, and, while in college, he totaled three of his father's cars. After college, he married and divorced "an older, alcoholic woman who had several children." He told me that he now knew that he was unable to make a stable relationship with any woman, so he only went with unsuitable women. Bill said that he never lied to nor did he make false promises to any of these women. As a young adult, Bill said he had used many street drugs, but that now he was only taking pills to sleep.

Bill denied having had any compulsions, but said that during his twenties, he had obsessed about whether or not he had impregnated his sister. Throughout his evaluation, he complained of depression and loneliness and cried sporadically. When I asked him, he said that he never had self-condemnatory nor self-destructive thoughts.

I concluded that Bill was sad, but not depressed or suicidal. He suffered from obsessions, a success neurosis, and a Madonna-Prostitute complex. I offered him a psychoanalytic treatment, but Bill said that his previous experiences with psychotherapists led him to fear that I would "keep him in treatment forever by gaining control over him," and that "further psychoanalysis would be a waste of his time." However, he tentatively agreed to try psychoanalysis five-times-a-week.

Only after he worked with me for five months was he able to tell me of his foot fetish. Hesitatingly, he revealed that, in order to have an orgasm, he had to either look at, or fantasy looking at, "a woman's skinny, pretty feet with long, painted toes."

COURSE OF THERAPY

During the beginning phase of his analysis, Bill tried to push me away by criticizing me. For example, he accused me of "scribbling my notes" or "walking ungracefully." I pointed this out and reminded him that he had told me that he had done similar things to push his mother away. Following this interpretation, Bill began to bring me personal gifts. I told him that if I accepted them, he could reject me for being unprofessional, and if I did not, he could reject me for spurning his offerings. With my help he came to understand that he had "played these games" with me to test if I could maintain what he had called an appropriate limit on our professional relationship. After I had passed his tests, he told me that his past analyst had also been the analyst of both of his parents. He said that this analyst had forfeited his professional integrity by becoming too personally involved with the family. Bill then became less resistant, relaxed, and began to freely associate.

Bill often turned around on the couch to look at me, and I would tell him that he was breaking the rules. Following one such session he reported a dream in which his *"mother was lying down and spreading her legs."* He had become frightened and woke up. He associated that he did not want to develop a positive relationship with me because I then *"might spread"* my *"legs."* Bill said that yesterday on the couch he had become frightened because he had become "intensely aware" of his penis and had the thought that he "wanted to fuck" me. He said that he then had to turn and look at me to be sure that I would not have intercourse with him, and that when I told him that he was breaking the rules, he had felt relieved. He then complained that his prior analysts had never faulted him when he broke their rules. I explained that thoughts were different from deeds and that with me he should verbalize his thoughts but not act on them. Bill said that he felt secure with me because I stuck to my "rules," but that sometimes he became intensely angry with me for being "too analytic" (i.e., too abstinent). At such times he felt that I did not care what happened to him, became angry at me, turned his anger inward against himself, and then developed various physical symptoms. He then went to medical specialists who found no physical causes for his symptoms. His grandfather then developed bladder cancer, and Bill developed urinary symptoms. A urologist found no physical abnormalities. Bill also turned his anger with me against himself by not wearing his helmet while riding his motorcycle. Bill then dreamed that he *"had a motorcycle accident."* We worked on the dream and he realized that he had been riding recklessly to try to induce me to show concern. Realizing this, he became aware that he had often gained his busy mother's attention by becoming injured or sick. The next session Bill came into my office, threw a helmet on the floor and told me that he was now wearing it. Bill was also turning his anger with me against himself by picking at his lip, fingers, mouth, or nose while on the couch. Later in his first year of psychoanalysis, we learned that this was a manifestation of his identification with his aggressive, foot and toe picking, mother.

Throughout the first part of his analysis, Bill consistently came to each session ten to fifteen minutes late. On arriving, he always threw his disheveled jacket on the floor. After several months, I pointed this out to him, and he again told me that his parents and former analysts were remiss for not having cared enough about him to set appropriate limits on his behavior. After we worked on his being late, he began to come on time and smiled as he hung up his jacket. Soon after this change, he told me that on those days that we did not meet, he felt "lonely and empty."

Following this, during the remainder of his first year of psycho-analysis, Bill recalled the following significant memories:

(1) When his mother started Bill in training pants, she said, "This is going to be difficult for you," and it was. His early aversion to defecating never went away. As a child he did not want to defecate anywhere but at home. He still does not want to defecate anywhere but at home.

(2) Every morning when he was a toddler, he watched his mother pull up her pretty nightgown, cross her legs, and pick her long skinny toes until they bled.

(3) When he was four and a half, his mother forgot to engage her cars' handbrake before she got out of the car, and the car rolled down a hill with only himself and his sister in it.

(4) Just before he was five, Bill walked in on his parents while they were having intercourse. His father calmly said, "Pull up a chair and watch," but Bill quickly left the room.

(5) When Bill was five, he was afraid of the dark, and he had two recurrent nightmares: I. *"I went down into a cave shaped like a cornu-copia. It got smaller and smaller."* II. *"I was indoors, floating up stairs."* Associations: "Sometimes I would get out of the cave and sometimes I would wake up before I got out."

(6) When six, Bill had a nightmare: *"A monster was coming after me, and I was defenseless."*

(7) Also at age six, his mother had told Bill to show his penis to his sister so that she would know what one looked like. After that, Bill frequently engaged in sexual play with his sister. When his parents found him examining his sister's vagina, they said nothing.

(8) Also when he was six, the female psychoanalyst that he was seeing told him that he could do whatever he wanted to do with her. He believed that this was a sexual solicitation and became frightened.

He refused to see her again. He then increased his sexual play with his sister, and began sticking his penis into her vagina.

(9) When he was seven, his mother confided to him that his father was having an affair with an attractive young woman.

(10) When he was nine, Bill began masturbating.

(11) From nine to eleven he worried that he might have impregnated his sister. He wrote notes to his father about his sexual activity with his sister, hoping that his father would tell him to stop. However, instead of telling him to stop, his father merely said that someday he (Bill) would "have a high time on the old town."

(12) When Bill was ten, his mother began to insist that he sit next to her at their formal dinners. Then, when Bill was fourteen, he told his mother that he did not want to sit next to her at the table any more because she "smelled badly."

(13) At age 14, Bill was still "messing around sexually" with his sister.

During his second year of analysis, Bill began taking college classes at night. Then he began to mismanage his finances and to do things either "at the wrong time or in the wrong place." During this time, he had many examination dreams. He also had dreams in which he inhibited himself, doubted, did and undid things, and shamed himself out of guilt. The following two dreams revealed that he doubted that psychoanalysis would help him: I. *"My phone went dead while I was dialing 911."* II. *"I had marbles in my ears that prevented me from hearing what you* [his analyst] *said."*

He also had a series of dreams in which *Monsters were trying to get him*. To these dreams he associated, "If the *monsters* don't *get me* in my dreams, my motorcycle will *get me* in real life. Mice (He called sexual thoughts, mice) are running around in my mind—and the mice ran over to the *farmer's wife*." I added, "And she cut off their tails with a carving knife." He replied, "Yes, if I succeed in college, the *farmer's wife* (his mother) will castrate me." He then remembered that at age eight, his (gentleman-farmer) father had yelled at his mother, "You can crush your son's balls, but not mine."

Bill was twenty minutes late to his next appointment and told me that he had dreamed: *"You* [me] *were poking a big piece of glass into my stomach. I picked out pieces of bloody glass and washed the blood off my feet with a hose."* He associated to his bad habit of picking his face and fingers until they bled, and then remembered that, when he was three to four years old, he had often watched his mother, in her pretty night-gown, cross her legs to pick her toes until they bled. He then recalled an aspect of these occurrences that he had formerly forgotten: He told me that he would be playing on the floor when his mother picked her toes, and that this let him view her exposed genitals. He saw that she lacked a penis and concluded that she must have picked off her penis like she was now picking off parts of her toes. After that, whenever he saw his mother picking her toes, he avoided looking at her genitals and deliberately concentrated his attention on her feet.

Bill then associated that in the dream he had symbolically castrated himself with the *piece of glass* to punish himself for the mice—that is, the sexual thoughts—that were running around in his mind.

That night Bill dreamed, "I was happy because you *were orchestrating my life.*" He associated that he wanted me to "eliminate his mice," by setting external limits on his sexual thoughts. Then, immediately after explaining to me how good he was at manipulating his mother to get money, he asked me to change his appointment times. Jokingly, I told him that if I were to change his appointment times, he might feel he had manipulated me like he had his mother, and then he might again become frightened of the mice running around in his head. He understood, and we laughed together.

Then Bill had a series of dreams about feet and about castration. In one dream *someone was mashing* red *grapes with her* feet. His associations to this dream led him to remember his having the early fantasy that his mother had picked on her penis until it bled and came off. He also had a dream about a *fish,* and another about *eviscerated chickens.* His associations to these two dreams revealed that they also represented castration. These castration dreams helped him understand that his current symptom of picking his fingers, mouth, and nose until they bled, represented his mother's picking her feet until they bled. This reassured him that his mother's genital area had healed, because his fingers, mouth, and nose always healed.

We analyzed many of his dreams. In some, *he would get close to me, become anxious, and then hostilely push me away.* In others, *he would first see me as sexually attractive and then see me as unattractive.* He also had many dreams in which I was half-Japanese and, therefore, unlike his mother. In one dream he punished himself for having sexual desires for me, by *driving on the wrong side of the road and having the police stop him.* In many dreams *he tried, but failed, to date attractive, thin, redheaded women like his mother.* In these dreams something always went wrong, such as *the lenses falling out of his glasses* or *his only having "half an erection."*

One time when he spoke of having sexual feelings for me, he became frightened and remembered having been frightened in the same way when he was fifteen:

His mother was confiding in him about her problems with his father. He tried to comfort her by kissing her passionately on the mouth. His sexual arousal surprised and frightened him. Several days later, his father teased him by telling him that he was lovesick for a girlfriend. Bill became so flustered that he tried to push his father down the stairs. If his father had not jumped out of the way, Bill said that he might have gotten rid of the competition. Instead, his father got rid of the competition by sending him off to a school. After recalling this event, Bill cried and said, "The following Christmas, my parents gave me an expensive gift. How could they give me something so nice after I had been so bad?"

Bill then had three dreams in which he was seeking external limits: (1) *He was drafted into the Army.* (2) *He was handcuffed.* (3) *He had a motorcycle that lacked a motor.*

He also had many dreams in which he shamed himself. Two examples are: (1) *people were laughing at him because he had no pants on,* and (2) *people were laughing at him because he made a mess by spilling food on himself.* He then realized that he had done poorly when he had worked for his father to elicit criticism from his father to shame himself for having been too close to his mother. Bill now understood that he still was looking for both limits and approval from his father.

During Bill's fourth year of analysis, he told me that he had always avoided looking at my feet and legs so that he would not get aroused, but that today he had looked and noticed a nevus on the back of my leg. He said that my nevus made him think of a vagina, and that naked feet reminded him of vaginas and turned him on sexually. He said that whenever he saw women with naked feet or in sandals, "the mice would begin to run again and drive him crazy."

In subsequent sessions, he reminisced about his mother having exposed her genitals while picking her feet. Each time he did, he said "the mice were running." As he worked on this, his sexual interest in women's feet diminished, and his sexual interest in women's genitals increased. He told me that he was getting closer to me, and loving me more. This frightened him, and he doubted—back and forth—Did I, or did I not, love him in return?

Occasionally during these sessions, Bill would become furious and would run out of his sessions early. Eventually, I asked him if he was becoming furious at me because I was not setting limits on his sexual feelings toward me by stopping his free associations—just like his mother had not set limits on his sexual feelings toward her by covering her genitals. He said, "yes," and said that because his mother did not stop herself from exposing her genitals, he had learned to stop himself from responding sexually when he saw them. I reminded him that he had also become angry and had run away when his father teased him about his girlfriend.

The next day, Bill again came to my office wearing putrid smelling, dirty clothing. I pointed this out. He realized that he was trying to alienate me by offending me like he had offended his mother by telling her that she smelled badly. This helped him understand how he had used feelings of disgust toward bad smells (a reaction-formation) to protect himself from his sexual feelings toward his mother, me, and other women. Next, Bill again recalled his having walked in on his parents while they were having intercourse. He now remembered that he had seen both his mother's painted toes and his father's buttocks. His next thought was that he would like to go to bed with me, and that he hoped that I would become angry with him for wanting to do so.

A few days later, Bill told me that as he followed me into my office, he had the thought that I was shapely. He then immediately thought, "Bite your tongue, or you might kiss her." He next debated whether or not he should have kissed his mother in the car when he was fifteen. This debate (doing and undoing) made Bill aware that this type of thinking had also occurred at age four, when he pondered over whether or not he should have put his arm in the lemonade. These associations led him to again worry about whether his thoughts were equivalent to deeds. He next remembered that his fear of his magical thinking began after he had wished to see his father argue with his mother, and it had happened.

After achieving these new insights, Bill began to miss his appointments with me and to argue with me to avoid dealing further with his sexual thoughts and feelings about me. Then in one session he showed me the new, loaded pistol that he had just purchased, and he told me that he had dreamed that he was *"killing a woman."* My telephone then rang and he became angry and said, "Shoot that doctor." I told him that if he did not get rid of this gun, I would stop seeing him. Bill replied that he was pleased that he could not push me away with threats, and that, unlike his mother, I maintained the boundary that I had set. The next day he showed me the bill of sale for his pistol. Bill then retested my integrity by offering me a book. He was relieved when I told him that he was testing me and that I would not take it. During the next session, as he came into my office, he stared brazenly at my feet. After laying down on the couch, he told me that my feet were ugly and disgusting, and that my shoes did not fit. I suggested that he might be having negative thoughts about my feet because he feared having positive sexual feelings for them and for me. In everyday language, I explained to him that he was first displacing his sexual desire from my genital area to my feet, and was then using reaction-formation to find my feet disgusting. He again recounted the episodes in which his mother had exposed her genitals while crossing her legs to pick her "long, skinny, bleeding feet." He recalled how he had diverted his gaze from her genitals—which disgusted him because she had no penis—to her feet, which disgusted him because they were bleeding. Bill recognized that he was now reenacting, with me, this experience he'd had with his mother, to avoid having any positive sexual interest in my genitals. He then said that he wished that his father had set a limit on his sexual impulses rather than telling him to "Pull up a chair and watch" and telling him to "play with his sister's titties." Bill also wished that his mother had not told him to show his penis to his sister.

Several sessions later, Bill dreamed *that he and I were fully clothed in his parents' bed, and that he was standing on his head.* Laughing, he associated that in the dream he was *standing on his head* so that, instead of looking down at my feet to avoid looking at my genitals, he was looking down at my genitals to avoid looking at my feet. He was pleased that he was now able to do this in his dream. He then was able to openly describe his sexual thoughts and feelings about both his mother and me without feeling either anxiety or guilt.

Bill told me that he got the top grade on a college test. After telling me that, he told me he that he was sexually excited and had thoughts of "fucking" me. His next thought was that "it" might really happen, and he became terrified. I again reminded him that in his unconscious he believed that having a thought was the same as it happening. He then recalled that whenever his mother had complimented him, he had felt guilty because he worried that she might like him better than his father. Several sessions later, Bill told me that, while studying, he had the fantasy that he lost control and "fucked" me. He then masturbated to get his mind off of sex so he could continue to study.

A few days, later Bill dreamed that *his father chased him out of the house because he was sloppily dressed*. He associated that he wished that his father had set limits on him, like I did when I told him to get rid of his guns. He regretted that, after he had tried to knock his father down the stairs, his father had sent him off to prep school instead of censuring him. He now clearly understood that he had learned to believe that his hostile and sexual impulses had magical power because, as a child, his parents had rarely reprimanded or punished him for them. He said that when he had tried to provoke his former psychoanalysts, they, like his parents, had never responded. I reminded him that, when he was a child, he had frequent, frightening nightmares of monsters that frightened and subdued him. I suggested that these dreams might have represented his wish that his parents had set limits on him.

Bill continued to expand his insight into his oedipal conflict and his castration anxiety. After Bill's father had a cancer removed, Bill dreamed that *he himself was dying of cancer*. Bill immediately realized that the dream was a wish to punish himself for having wished his father dead. Bill said that he knew he was much better, because he could now study for four to five hours without becoming distracted.

He soon graduated from college with high grades, and he started a profitable business. These achievements did not make him anxious, as they would have before his psychoanalysis. His anxiety over his sexual feelings toward me had diminished, and he courted and married a "nice" woman—one who was not "down and out." She was not petite like his mother, and she had "pretty feet." They had intercourse infrequently, and when they did, he still had to fantasy a "disorganized woman" to achieve an orgasm. His orgasms were often premature. Two years after they married, they had a daughter.

After a session in which I had made an interpretation that he construed to be placing a limit on him, he was able to have a dream in which *he successfully took over his father's business, and it prospered*. However, he then partially had to undo his success in the dream *by forming a co-op that distributed all the earnings to his employees*.

Bill now understood that, when he was a child, he had felt that he could do whatever he wished to do by easily manipulating his parents.

This had led him to believe that he had magical omnipotent power, which both pleased and frightened him. He also understood that he was now defensively projecting his anger, which he felt had omnipotent power, onto a potential earthquake that would damage a nuclear power plant and release massive nuclear fallout. Although he knew that his fear was exaggerated by his residual neurosis, he still felt compelled to move away.

At his daughter's second birthday party, Bill had played a game of "pinching bugs" with her. He had pinched and tickled her gently around her legs and arms, and she had giggled. Later, she came from behind him and pinched him hard. Reflexly, without thinking or looking, he swung around and hit her too hard. She cried, and he felt horrible. His wife tried to reassure him by saying that smacking someone reflexively when you get pinched was normal. This led him to have the thought that if hitting his daughter was normal, having sex with her might also be normal. He then wondered what good it would do to move his daughter away from the nuclear power plant if his daughter was not safe with him. Could he make himself safe? He said that he did not feel worthy of my time and that I should help someone more worthy than he. I reminded him that he had told me that when he was fifteen, he had kissed his mother sensuously and had subsequently almost pushed his father down the stairs. Instead of punishing or reprimanding him for this behavior, his parents had rejected him by sending him away. I told him that now, like then, he was ready to go away rather than setting a limit on himself. He said that the pain of having hit his daughter was helping him to be a father and mother to himself.

In his tenth year of psychoanalysis, Bill was planning to move away to an area that did not have either earthquakes or nuclear power plants. He felt that his daughter was more important than he was and that he was finding the perfect place to nurture and educate her. We set a termination date. During the last two months of his analysis, we again worked-through many of his problems—especially his relationship with his parents, the development of his foot fetish, and his sexual and aggressive thoughts toward his daughter.

His sexual feelings no longer frightened him, but at times he would avoid his daughter because he had sexual feelings for her—just as at times he had avoided his sister and mother because he had sexual feelings for them. Bill was no longer abstaining from having intercourse with his wife. He no longer had premature ejaculations, and he did not have to think of women's feet or "down and out" women to be able to have an orgasm. He had come to realize that, when he had intercourse more often with his wife, his sexual feelings for his daughter ceased. He also learned that his fear that an earthquake might kill his daughter was partly a displacement of the unconscious anger and jealousy that he had had toward his sister.

He diligently set external limits on his daughter so that she would not fear her omnipotent wishes. He also remembered that when he had accomplished something, his father had told him that "anybody could have done that," and his mother had said "you could have done better," so he recognized his daughter's achievements and complimented her on them.

It was now clear to Bill that his castration anxiety began when he watched his mother pick her bleeding feet and saw that she had no penis. This castration anxiety intensified when he saw a dog bite off a part of his father's toe.

Bill felt that the insights he obtained from his analysis gave him "real" rather than "magical" power, and he hoped he could be a more successful father and businessman than his father had been. Bill felt good that he was successfully completing his analysis and was proud that he was moving to a place where he knew his business would thrive. He said that losing me would be devastating and that he did not want to face it. When I asked if Portland was really so dangerous a place to live, he replied that he knew that the danger was partly within his head for he had irrationally feared that he might lose control of his sexual or hostile impulses.

Bill understood his intense, conflicted, mother transference that he had toward me. He realized that if I said something to him, he felt I was controlling; whereas if I did not, he felt I was not paying enough attention to him. Although he had received increased attention from his mother by being injured or ill, he learned that he did not need to be injured or ill to get more attention either from me or his wife. He also realized that his feeling that I wanted him to remain dependent on me and not leave was the result of his transferring some of his parents' attitudes onto me.

That his mother liked to exhibit her body and get people to look at her was now clear to him. He clearly understood that she had not shown appropriate restraint when she exhibited her genitals. Because she had identified with her children, she had tried to give them the gratification that she felt she had missed by not setting limits on them. "Children," he said, "need to be taught to control their sexuality and aggression so they can fit into society and be comfortable with themselves." It was now time, Bill said, for him to use the knowledge and self-confidence that he had gained from his psychoanalysis.

During his last session, Bill said that he was no longer afraid of the magical power of his sexual or hostile wishes. Proudly, he said that he was happy with his new family and with our "good work together." He said he would write and tell me how he was doing.

As we said goodbye, he held my hand firmly.

Although Bill had completely worked through his conflicted sexual impulses, and had recovered from his fetishistic behavior, he was aware that he had not completely worked through his conflicted aggressive impulses.

Follow-ups four and ten years after he finished, revealed that Bill was operating a successful business in his new location. Bill said that his wife was a "gem" and that their marriage was fulfilling. He said that he no longer had a desire to look at women's feet, nor did he take a special interest in his wife's feet. He "enjoyed her entire body." He stressed that his daughter was the "joy of his life," and that he and his wife were setting firm, loving limits on her.

DISCUSSION: SUMMARY OF
BILL'S PSYCHODYNAMICS

The psychoanalysis of Bill's transference reactions made him aware that his parents had failed to give him external limits that he could internalize so that he could control his own impulses and wishes. He learned that his parents' permissiveness had fostered both his magical thinking and his fear of retaliatory castration.[1] He also became conscious of two formerly repressed events that had occurred during his fifth year of life. He came to understand that the following two experiences had led him to develop both his foot fetish and his neurotic symptoms:

(1) Bill saw his mother's genitals while she was "picking" her bleeding feet, and he displaced his *sexual interest and excitement* from her

---

[1]Novick, J., Novick, K.K. (1991) observed that a false sense of omnipotence of thought and deed constitutes a prominent component of the sexually deviant person's resistance (p. 307).

genitalia to her feet. After that, he became sexually aroused by "pretty" female feet and not by female genitalia.[2]

(2) Bill walked in on his parents while they were having intercourse and, from his position at the bottom of their bed, he saw his father's penis, that his mother lacked a penis, and his mother's feet. Although he wished to displace his father and take his father's place with his mother, he feared that his father might "pick off" his penis.

Following these two events Bill used his fetishistic behavior, his obsessive-compulsive defense mechanisms, and his success neurosis to protect his parents from his oedipal wishes and to protect himself from castration.

Thus, through his psychoanalysis, Bill gained insight that permitted him to resolve his intrapsychic conflicts and achieve mature adult gratification in both his love life and in his work.

This case bears out Freud's conclusions about fetishistic behavior (see chapter 1).

REFERENCES

GREENACRE, P. (1955). Further Considerations Regarding Fetishism. *Psychoanalytic Study of the Child* 10:187–194.

NOVICK, J. & NOVICK, K.K. (1991). Some Comments on Masochism and the Delusion of Omnipotence from a Developmental Perspective. *Journal of the American Psychoanalytic Association* 39:307–331.

---

[2] Greenacre (1955) considered that early exposure of adult genitals to a child, if repeated almost constantly, can lead to attitudes of great interest and confusion. Greenacre concluded that this kind of trauma is important as a predisposing factor in sexual deviations if it occurs between the second and fourth years of life in children. This trauma, Greenacre said, is significant depending on the degree to which the child is overwhelmed by it and resorts to fantasy or denial of reality to deal with the panic. The fetish, she said, fulfills this condition admirably.

TREATMENT OF A TRANSVESTITE
WOMAN-ABUSER

PRESENTING PROBLEM

John, a thirty-nine-year-old engineer and father of three children, ages seven, five, and three, complained that he constantly felt anxious, depressed, and was easily provoked to anger—especially by his wife. He said that his anger was childish and unwarranted, and that each time he lost his temper and struck his wife, he felt unkind, embarrassed, and totally unworthy of her affection. He feared that if he did not stop beating her, she would carry out her threat to leave him. In an attempt to avoid his fear of losing her, he immersed himself in his work, but at work his anger pushed away his coworkers and hampered his efficiency. His fear of abandonment by his wife and coworkers reminded him of how badly he had felt when he was five-years-old and his father—a very inhibited, quiet, passive man—divorced his mother and left the family. John did not see his father again until John was thirty-years-old. John's mother had been ashamed of the divorce and had coerced John into telling everyone that his father had been killed in the war. John recalled that he had also felt ashamed that he did not have a loving mother and father like other children. Recently, after an argument with his wife, John dreamed that he was *blowing up their kitchen*. John then recalled that as a child, after he heard his mother berating his passive father in their kitchen, he fantasied that *the kitchen might blow up*. He said he sought my help because he felt depressed over his difficulties with his wife and coworkers.

Initial Evaluation

After his parents' divorce, John, an only child, and his mother lived with mother's "stubborn, strict, and highly disciplined" parents. His mother was a "strict, meticulous, uncompromising university professor." She would criticize John, and then cover up her criticisms by telling him that she had "just been teasing." She was "always depressed" and, when he was naughty, she often withdrew to her room or left the house. When this happened, John felt rejected, and he had trouble curbing his anger. Like John's father, his mother's father was passive. He bragged that he never lost control. Instead, he was described as being passive-aggressive.

John's mother always dressed seductively and paid careful attention to John's eating and bowel habits. While at his grandmother's house his mother would make what she called "romantic spaghetti dinners for just the two of them." During these dinners John had "sexual feelings for her" and felt "bad for having them." He also remembered that when he was a young boy, he would sit on the toilet and watch his mother take a bath. He saw that she lacked a penis and that her "front bottom was red." He assumed that she was bleeding, and he became upset.

When his mother left him at home with his grandmother, he would forlornly ask her, "When is mommy coming back to monkey." "Monkey" was his mother's disapproving and disparaging nickname for him. John often put a stop to the disciplinary restrictions his mother put on him by pretending he was sorry and by acting sweetly toward her. When John became a teenager, his mother disciplined him by withholding money.

Although John's grandmother had told him that women who wore lipstick were hussies, in high school he became sexually aroused by girls who wore lipstick. He would fantasy kissing a girl and getting lipstick on his lips. Although he found football boring and feared he would get hurt, he played on the high school football team to prove that he was not small or inadequate. He felt sad because his mother never attended any of these games, or any of his school activities. Immediately after telling me this, he told me how terribly perturbed he had become when he witnessed his mother rejecting a sobbing boyfriend. Soon after John left home for college, his mother left her parent's home and remarried.

John attended an excellent college and did extremely well scholastically. However, he could not get along with many of the women he dated. In his third year of college he proposed marriage to a classmate. She rejected him, and he gave her a black eye. She complained to the school authorities, and he was expelled. This made him feel ashamed and worthless. His mother told him that he was treated unfairly. Then John worked for a year, and was then accepted into another excellent college where he graduated with high honors. He obtained an excellent job and began dating a "sympathetic, supportive, understanding woman" upon whom he soon "became very dependent." They were married, and the "stability, security, and support" he received from his wife helped him do well in his job. After they had three children, John began to lose his temper easily with her and abuse her physically. Eventually, she told him that if he did not stop, she would divorce him. Overwrought at the prospect of losing his family, John sought my help and accepted my recommendation that he begin a psychoanalysis.

It was not until his twelfth psychoanalytic session that John sheepishly told me things that he had not told me before. He said that in adolescence he had begun to put on his mother's underclothing, look at himself in a mirror, and masturbate, and that he was now doing the same thing with his wife's underclothing.

COURSE OF THERAPY

Initial Psychoanalytic Sessions

John complained that his mother had dominated and controlled him. She had insisted that he be punctual and polite. She demanded that he urinate to the side of the toilet bowel, because "gentlemen do not make noise when they urinate." His grandmother told him that if he did not urinate when she told him to, his urine would get into his blood and kill him. She also frightened him by warning him not to get into strangers' cars, because he would get kidnapped like his mother had been when she was a teenager. Every morning, both his mother and his grandmother put pieces of Ivory Soap up his anus, and insisted that he defecate. After he did defecate, they meticulously cleaned his anus. After the age of five, this made him feel babyish and inadequate. One time, John's grandmother caught him masturbating with soap in the bathtub, and she told him that if he played with his penis, it would fall off. For several days after that, he feared that it would fall off. Another time, his grandmother found him making an airplane by putting a toy propeller into the meatus of his penis. She told him that they would have to "cut it out," and he thought she meant "cut out his penis." For several days after that, his penis burned when he urinated, and he feared that his penis would fall off.

John's mother bathed and slept with him until he was five. Once while he was in the tub with her, she showed him her Caesarian scar and told him that it was the result of his birth. He saw her bleeding vulva and fantasied that her menstrual blood was also the consequence of his birth. Since then he has avoided looking at "women's bottoms."

As he got older, John found his mother's perfume, sensuous voice, and tight clothing flirtatious and arousing.

During latency, John believed that babies were born through the rectum, and he had night dreams of *touching his mother's breast* and of *putting female genitalia onto a male*. During adolescence, he began to have fantasies of having anal intercourse with women.

Although John weighed only 120 pounds in high school, he felt he had to be tough. He played varsity football and felt he was a great football player whenever he tackled a 160-pound opponent. I asked him if his wife or his mother appreciated his achievements. John said that they did not. Instead, they became jealous, and this upset him. When John was eighteen, he felt that—although his mother spoke with great authority—she was not always reliable.

First Year of His Psychoanalysis

John free-associated easily, regressed rapidly, and his conflicts emerged. This made him anxious, and he then began to act out by becoming even more angry and verbally abusive to his female colleagues and more physically abusive to his wife. He also withheld money from his wife and threatened to leave her. I told him, repeatedly, that he was doing to his female colleagues and wife what his mother and grandmother had done to him. John then transferred his anger onto me. He accused me of being "competitive," "angry," "double-binding," and "non-caring." Forcefully, he told me that he had no "positive, loving, feelings" for me. Eventually, however, John realized that he was diverting the anger that he had originally felt toward his mother onto me, and he also became aware that, to reduce his anxiety, he had inhibited his "tender, positive feelings" toward me. He then became aware that he had both hateful and loving feelings toward his mother, and that he had been projecting both his idealized, good mother image and his belittling, bad mother image onto his wife, other women, and me. He then recognized that whenever he had felt close to me, he had become anxious, for he feared that I would withdraw from him like his mother had.

John then began to tell me that my silent, withdrawn analytic posture made him feel rejected. Once, I was five minutes late to his session, and he told me that I had come late because I was angry with him, and that I should admit and confess that I was angry. With my help, he then recalled that when his mother was angry with him, she would often come late, be silent, and tell him that she "never got angry." John then was able to see that he was transferring both his mother's anger—and her denial of her anger—onto me, like he had done with his former girlfriends and his wife. He recalled that when his mother was angry with his behavior, she often shamed him by telling him, "No son of mine would have done that." As John became more aware of his tendency, both to see me as his degrading mother and to degrade me, he became less withholding and more aware of his repressed thoughts and feelings of shame.

Several weeks later, John asked me to "cancel" an appointment. I did. He then became enraged because I did not know that when he said "cancel" he meant "change." He then realized that he had difficulty asking people to change appointment times because his mother had refused to change her schedule to accommodate him. Gradually, John became consciously aware of his formerly unconscious identification with his hostilely aggressive mother.

Not until his fourth year of psychoanalysis did John become aware that he had been unconsciously equating my rule that he free-associate to his mother's demands for him to produce feces when she put soap into his anus. This had caused him to resist free-associating as he had resisted defecating. As John achieved these new insights, he began to give more of his income to his family and to get along better with both his male and female colleagues.

John's conflict over whether to stay close to me or separate from me now became a recurrent theme in his free associations. He learned that when he felt close to me in the mother-transference, he became anxious because he feared that I would withdraw from him like his mother often had. Early in his treatment, John believed that his mother was usually available to him. Later, he realized that she had spent most of her time alone in her third floor bedroom. When he was needy or ill, it was his grandmother, not his mother, who came to him. At those times he would cry and ask his grandmother, "Will mommy come to monkey?"

John became very depressed during the middle phase of his psychoanalysis. He realized that he was putting himself down in the same way that his mother had put down both himself and his father. John then figured out that his mother had compensated for her feelings of shame by disparaging and competing with males. He became aware that he had adapted to this behavior by concealing his ambitions and achievements from her and by shaming himself. Once he understood this, he was able to tell me that he had graduated at the top of his class in college. John was then also able to reevaluate his attitude toward his father. John had often felt anger at his father for not being there for him, but he now suspected that his early relationship with his father might not have been so bad as his mother had portrayed it. Tearfully, he recalled that his father had always sent him birthday and Christmas gifts, which his mother had disparaged. Because John always got on well with men, he surmised that he might have had a good relationship with his father.

Regressing further in his psychoanalysis, John began battling with me for control. He would stop free associating, attack me verbally, or threaten to "stop coming." These behaviors became a useful indication that he was trying to avoid recalling some anxiety-provoking unconscious memory that was threatening to come into consciousness. For example, he told me that he could no longer afford to be in psychoanalysis because he had purchased an expensive horse. He went on to tell me that the horse's manure was offending his neighbors. Then he remembered that he had exasperated his mother by coming to her with his "pants full of shit" while she had guests and was trying to be a "perfect, hostess."

If John's wife or I planned to be away, he would conceal his separation anxiety behind his anger. For example, when his wife was about to leave on a trip, he provoked a fight with her and hit her as he would have liked to have hit his mother. Once, when both his wife and I were about to be away, John became silent on the couch. I asked him what he was thinking. He banged on my wall, jumped up, said that he had to leave, and ran from my office. Later that day, I phoned him at work, and asked if he had left me before I could leave him. He was surprised and pleased, both that I called him and that I could talk so calmly about his expression of anger. He said that my calmness made it possible for him to tell me that he had run away because he had feared that he might hit me for being about to leave him. The following day he brought in two dreams. In the first one: *He was a small boy looking down onto the street from a second story window. He watched his wife, who was all dressed up, going out the door and getting into her car. Then, magically, he was in her car defecating.* In the second dream: *A lady doctor phoned him.* Associating to these dreams, John realized that *he felt that his wife and I were leaving him, because we thought that he was "smelly, shitty, and unlovable—just like he had felt that his mother had left him because she thought he was "smelly, shitty, and unlovable."* Once John knew that he had run out of my office because he felt shame and anger over his helpless-dependent feelings of loneliness and sadness, he had the impulse to smear my crayons all over my office walls. John then said that he now understood that in addition to feeling angry that I was leaving him, he also felt guilty for being angry. He now again recalled sitting on the toilet and, while crying, asking his grandmother "Will mommy come home to monkey?"

Regressing further in the transference, John attempted to get me to feel the shame and pain that he had experienced as a child. He would insult me, yell at me, say that psychoanalysis was "a pile of bullshit," and threaten to quit and leave me. As a further resistance, John then displaced this anger from me onto his wife. After I interpreted this acting out behavior, he settled down, and we worked on his anger over his separation from, and loss of, his mother. For example, I had to cancel a session. John felt abandoned and rejected, and stopped coming to his sessions. I telephoned him and reminded him that he was breaking our analytic contract. He returned and told me that he was surprised that I had chased after him and that "perhaps" that might mean that I cared about him. For him, this was a corrective emotional experience. He noted that whenever he had withdrawn from his mother, she had never pursued him, and this had made him feel abandoned and rejected. Then, at the end of the session, when he sat up on the couch to leave, he looked at my face and said that he was both surprised and pleased to see that I did not have a "hostile, shit-eating grin on my face"—like his mother would have had. Instead, he saw a look of concern. John remembered that during his latency years he had "felt like a dog" when his mother had called him for dinner with a dog whistle. If he did not come immediately—instead of pursuing him—she would lock him out of the house.

John told me that during the times he had felt rejected by me, he had had intercourse with a colleague. He gradually understood that this behavior repeated his having turned to his "good grandmother" when he felt rejected by his "bad mother." As John gradually came to understand that, unlike his mother, I did not put him down or reject him for being masculine, his sexual acting out gradually diminished. John then, gingerly, began to talk to me about his masculine sexual feelings for me. He told me that he felt less masculine whenever his wife or I left him or he felt that either of us had withdrawn from him emotionally. He also noted that it was at these times that he would put on women's clothing to masturbate. Eventually, he realized that when he cross-dressed and looked at himself in a mirror, he was imagining he saw the image of the woman that he felt he had lost. In other words, when a woman he loved, left him, he would preserve her image by putting on clothing similar to hers and looking at himself in a mirror. Thus, he was identifying with a lost love object. He noted that after masturbating while wearing his wife's clothing and looking into a mirror, he would always become unreasonably angry with himself. He now realized that this anger actually belonged to his wife. Our subsequent psycho-analytic work together revealed other unconscious determinants of his cross-dressing.

John dreamed that *I had long hair*. He associated that, although he had noticed that I had cut off my long hair three months ago, he delib-erately had not mentioned it. In the past John had always compliment-ed me on any change in my appearance. This dream led John to remem-ber that when he was a boy, his mother had insisted that he notice and compliment her on any change in her appearance. If he did not, she became offended and criticized him. John said that he deliberately avoided mentioning my haircut because he no longer wanted to please his mother. John said that he was testing me to see if I would become offended—like his mother would have been. He added that he feared that if he agreed with everything I said, and complimented my appear-ance, he would no longer exist with a separate identity. He feared get-ting sucked into my world like he had been sucked into his mother's world. John said that he found himself fantasying that he was arguing against my potential objections when he decided to do something self-destructive, just like he had argued with his mother's objections to his doing anything independently.

John dreamed that *his wife was in her car and was about to leave, and he "pissed" in her car*. He associated that in the dream his wife represented his mother, and that he pissed in her car to thwart her demand that he sit down to urinate. He then recalled that as a child when his mother drove them on trips, she had him urinate out the car door. If he aimed his stream too high and made it go too far, his mother would criticize him. He next recalled the dream in which he was defe-cating into his wife's car.

I told John that when he had competed with, degraded, mocked, or abused his wife or me, he was doing to us what his mother had done to him—and what he had wanted to do to his mother. John acknowledged that my interpretation was accurate, and he felt awful that he had been discharging the anger that he had felt toward his mother onto his wife and me. He then also became aware that he had been withdrawing from his wife and from me just like his mother had withdrawn from him. John was then able to empathize with how his wife and I felt when he was either hostile toward us or withdrawn from us. He was now consciously aware of his having identified with the often-lost object—his mother.

With my help, John learned that he had become angry with and fought with his wife or me whenever he felt inadequate and helpless—like he had felt as a child with his mother and grandmother. He also realized that he had not learned to control his anger as a child, because his mother and grandmother had not disciplined him with external limits. Instead, they had shamed him. He said that, as a child, when he had temper tantrums, he tried to discipline himself by banging his head. Soon John became aware that he no longer felt like an inadequate, helpless little boy who needed someone to set external limits on his anger. He did not want to lose his wife and children so he resolved to stop discharging his past anger toward his mother onto others. John progressively became more affectionate toward his wife, and became able to tell her that he loved her. He consciously used great effort to control his anger and discharge it more appropriately. This was difficult for him because expressing loving feelings, unconsciously made him feel that he was complying with his mother's wishes. This was also difficult for him because he felt that if he expressed loving feelings, he would lose his masculine identity. John resolved to no longer shame or harm himself.

John complained that his mother had often told him that she was "sorry" when she was not. I explained to him that her apologies were most likely reaction-formations to cover up her residual hostility toward him. He replied that he must have unconsciously known that, because he has never been able to say he was "sorry" to anyone.

Now that John was aware that he had transferred the feelings he had toward his mother onto his wife, and me, he saw the many ways in which his wife and I differed from his mother. He laughed and said that he loved his wife's laxness and sloppiness. This joking with me was something new. It indicated that both his observing ego and our working-alliance had improved. John said that he now understood that unconsciously he had chosen a woman analyst so that he could work on his hostility toward women.

John now recognized that he had made many different identifications with his mother, which he had acted out by doing to his wife and me what his mother had done to him. For example, he had always hated his mother for constantly cleaning up behind him. Now he was constantly provoking his wife by always cleaning up after her. John was also identifying with his mother's having "stuck soap up his ass," when he bought his wife a dildo and wanted to "stick it up her ass." John now also understood why he had often become self critical and depressed without knowing why. This had happened whenever he found himself behaving like his mother. I explained to him that he had become depressed because he was turning the anger he felt toward his mother inward toward the mother he had internalized.

While his wife and children were away on a trip, John prepared a welcome-home dinner for them. While doing so, he recalled the pleasure he had experienced when he helped his grandmother in the kitchen. He then remembered that he first put on women's clothing to masturbate immediately after his grandmother's death. The following night, he dreamed that *he felt anxious and had to pick out his own men's pants from a pile of other men's and women's clothing.*

John's hostile mother transference toward his wife and other women, then, gradually decreased, but his hostile mother transference toward me intensified. He fantasied leaving a smelly, fecal mess in my bathroom and imagined that a car would hit me and he would need to find a new psychoanalyst. He complained that I demanded too much, and that I did not appreciate his free associations. If I said anything, he would become angry and withholding. He criticized my clothing and feared that I would retaliate. John became increasingly aware that this anger was inappropriate and said that he was jealous of my husband and had positive, sexual feelings for me. He said he was suppressing these feelings because he did not want to become dependent on me as he had been on his mother. John then dreamed that *he was a little boy, and that Professor Freud was on the floor, coaxing him away from his mother.* He associated that the male doctor in the dream represented his wish that a male doctor would intervene and protect him from his sexual wishes for me—like he had wished that his father had been there to intervene and protect him from his sexual feelings for his mother. He worried that I would become depressed if he were away, like he wished his mother would have been. John then fantasized rescuing me from my depression, just as he had tried to rescue his mother from her depressions. He said that he was able to share with me his negative and positive feelings toward me, because he now felt that he could trust me.

John said that although he knew that I was working hard to concentrate on and remember what he was saying, he felt critical of me for telling him to postpone making major decisions until he better understood his conflicts. John then dreamed that *he gave me smelly fish and a man's dirty shoe.* He associated that these objects represented fecal penises. He thought that he had made the fish smelly and the shoe dirty to see if I would tolerate his penis. In another dream *he gave me male genitalia.* This dream was evidence of both his wish to see me in a father role and his wish to give his mother the penis that she wanted, but lacked.

John told me that each time that I had canceled a session he had felt pressured to put on his wife's clothing to masturbate. He next associated to the nursery rhyme, "Peter, Peter Pumpkin Eater had a Wife and Couldn't Keep Her." John recognized that this association expressed his wish to incorporate me orally and "keep me in a pumpkin shell so he could keep me very well." The night after he made this associative connection, he dreamed that *I was deformed and smelly.* He associated that he wished that I would accept his [anal] aggression and not leave him as his father had. His ambivalent wishes, both to keep me and to deform me, were now very conscious. He said that he had withheld some of his thoughts from me so that he would not become a reflection of me—like he had become a reflection of his mother. John again expressed anal aggression by having a thought of messing in my bathroom—just like he had messed his mother's bathroom when he was a child to upset her. Although John wanted me to set limits by charging him money, he said that it was an injury to his self-esteem that I did charge him money. John then said that he wished to see his father.

Later, while visiting his mother, John watched her wipe her dog's anus after it defecated, and he felt angry that his mother had continued to wipe his bottom until after he was five. It meant to him that she thought that he could not do it for himself. He recognized that most of his early memories involved his mother's handling of his bowel functions and that her anal intrusiveness had resulted in his ritualistic bowel habits, his low self-esteem, and his aggressive attitude toward women.

"If I am hostile," he said, "I don't have to think about sexuality, so my bitching and fussing became a way of life."

Although John was now very aware that his hostile attitude toward women originated from his conflict with his mother and grandmother about his bowel functions, he had not yet faced or dealt with his oedipal issues.

We interrupted therapy over the Christmas holiday. When we resumed, John said that during the break he had to work hard to control his anger, and he had worked on his identification with his mother's hostility. He complained that his mother expressed her anger unconsciously by letting him wait for the school bus in the freezing cold, and by never greeting him or hugging him when he came home from school. She treated her own father badly, and said negative things about him. John said that because his mother was never aware of her own anger, she could not help him with his. It was now apparent to him that his mother had trouble separating from her parents and becoming an individual. She could not mother, he concluded, because she had not been mothered.

He dreamed that *he was sitting on a sofa with a woman. She had no pants on, and he saw her pelvic area. He tried to pull her dress down, because if he were caught looking at her, his wife would be angry.* This dream reminded him that his mother had worn negligees around the house when he was small. He concluded that she did not even know that she was being seductive to him. He thought of the many ways that she had hurt him without knowing it. John empathetically said that his wife also hurt him because she too had problems. He vowed to stop putting his mother onto his wife and feeling rejected when his wife needed to be alone. John then dreamed that *he was competing with me.* He associated that his mother and grandmother had always said, "Don't get too big for your britches." Sarcastically, he said that he never heard them say, "Don't get too big for your skirt."

Now that he was aware that his angry feelings belonged mostly to his mother, he no longer needed to act them out on others. He now knew that both his mother and his wife obtained gratification by provoking him to act out their own angry feelings. However, like he had learned to do with me, he was now putting his anger toward his wife into words instead of beating her. For example, he took his children horseback riding, one fell off, and was hurt. His wife became enraged and blamed him. Although he became angry, he was able control himself and talk with her. John then **dreamed** that *he was on my couch, and I was holding his hands down to control his rage so that he would not hit me.*

Second and Third Year of His Psychoanalysis

One month later, John dreamed: *he was walking into a long narrow bathroom. A male high-school friend of his was wearing pantyhose. So John thought that it was okay for him to also put on pantyhose. It was exciting. The pantyhose needed to be washed. So John took a shower and he had an orgasm.* The evening before the dream he had expressed anger toward his wife for carelessly leaving her panty hose out where he could see them. Actually, he was not angry with her for leaving them out, but was angry because he was tempted to put them on when he saw them. He had not put on his wife's clothing for a long time. He felt bad for having tried to control her with anger, because his mother always tried to control him with anger. This episode also made it clear to him that he had identified with his mother's compulsive neatness. John then remembered that his mother had washed and hung her stockings over the shower every evening and that this had enticed him to put them on to masturbate. This had made him feel ashamed and guilty.

A week later, John became very angry with me for wearing a pair of stockings with seams down the back. He said his mother always wore that kind of stockings, which had turned him on when he saw her compulsively straightening the seams. The next night he **dreamed** that *my husband died of cancer, and I became a woman without a husband—just like his mother.*

A few weeks later, I was wearing open heeled shoes. John said that he became sexually aroused because my shoes made my calves and rump look more attractive. Then he attempted to provoke an argument with me about some trivial matter and said that he did not want to come to his next session. He immediately recognized that he had tried to provoke an argument with me to defend against his having sexual feelings for me—just like he had argued with his mother to defend against his having sexual feelings for her. John said that he felt like calling me a "bitch," even though I was unlike his mother and he could trust me with his "cock."

John asked himself what made him decide to marry his wife. He said it was because she was from a good family and because, although she knew he had given his girlfriend a black eye, his wife was still supportive and said that he was a nice guy whom she was happy to be with. John said he had not been aware of how inadequate he had been feeling for most of his life.

John said that he was now beginning to feel that I was less like his mother and more like his father.

Four months later, John asked me to change an appointment time. I did so readily. He then said that he had been afraid to ask me because he had anticipated that I would refuse, and had become angry with me. John then told me that he was angry with me for passively allowing him to "mess up" my schedule. I interpreted to him that he was angry with me for passively running away from the conflict he had imagined that he had with me over our schedule—like he had been angry with his father for passively running away from the conflict he had with John's mother. I suggested that he might want me to become the aggressive father he did not have. He agreed, and, laughing, said that he wished that his father had shown him how to be appropriately aggressive.

John's grandfather died, and John became depressed and self-depreciatory. I explained to him that he was turning against himself the anger that he had felt toward both his grandfather and his father for leaving him. His depression then lifted.

John fantasied that he was taking me with him to work and remembered that as a boy he had similar fantasies of taking his mother with him. He then remembered that as a boy he would fantasy that he would grow up fast and marry his mother before she got too old for him and before she married someone else. He then began to talk about how frustrating vacations had been with her. John then became hostile toward me and abruptly left in the middle of our session. I followed him out the door, and urged him to come back. He did, and told me that my coming after him was a rare and pleasant experience because no one else had ever cared enough to chase after him. John told me that he had run out of our session because he had become afraid of his anger toward me. He said that actually his anger had not been toward me, but had been toward his mother who had frustrated him on these vacations.

A few weeks later, John fell off a horse and was pleased that he had not blamed either the horse or himself. He said, "If something went wrong, my mother's always had to blame someone else or something else and not herself. I'm glad that I'm outgrowing the mother part of me that I don't like." Thus, John's observing ego was continuing to develop, and he realized that much of the anger that he was now feeling and expressing toward both his wife and me, actually belonged to his mother because she had made him feel dirty and unwanted.

John's mother was about to visit, and he became anxious. He said he wanted to put his head in my lap and be comforted by the warmth of my body. He fantasied that he would also like to be close to my husband, for he saw us as "good parents." John then said that he would like to end his analysis with me, and start a new one with a male analyst—because he would not get sexual feelings for a man. However, he worried that he might have more castration fears with a male analyst.

John said that while his mother was visiting she "stomped around" his house wearing only her stockings and a slip—just like she had when he was growing up. She doted on his daughter, slighted his older son, and spent much time in the bathroom watching and washing his younger son. John disregarded this behavior until he saw her putting women's hair spray onto his son's hair. Then John became incensed and remembered that when he was five, his mother would spit on his hair to make it stay in place. He then associated that she did this because she did not want anything to "stick out" on boys, and he told his mother to stop controlling and emasculating his son. Later, when his mother told him that she was ashamed because he was in psychoanalysis, he angrily reprimanded her. John noted that while he was reprimanding her, he had the wish to have anal intercourse with some woman. He soon realized that this wish represented a way to retaliate against his mother for having shoved slivers of soap up his anus. During the visit, "he tried to be as good as she thought he should be," but he actually "competed with her by trying to be better than she."

Following his mother's visit, when his wife provoked him, he was able to refrain from physically assaulting her, but, occasionally, he still vented his anger toward her verbally. He remembered that in adolescence he had moved to a bedroom, far from his mother's bedroom, and now realized that his erotic feelings for her had upset him. After he changed bedrooms, she told him that when she was gone, he would be sorry.

John's wife told him that she had learned that when she disagreed with him she should not confront him because if she did, he would either abuse her or leave the house. He had done the same thing to his friends, coworkers, and to me. Often when I had confronted John, he had run out of my office. Therefore, I also had learned to be careful when confronting him. I decided to now begin to confront him more directly, so that he could experience and learn to handle his anger. The first time I did this, and he became angry, John told me that he did not want to listen to me, and said that if my voice got any louder, his would get even louder. He then got off the couch and said that he was tired of "fighting" with me. I asked why he could not "disagree" with me? He angrily replied, "No way!" and he abruptly ran out of my office.

The next day, John told me that he had taken flight because he had "heard anger in my voice" and felt that I was "deliberately provoking" him into a "fight." He said that when he left the session, he felt like his "mother had reprimanded him," and that I was like his mother, who had always said she was "never angry," and always acted as though she was "absolutely flawless." He then demanded that I "admit" that I was angry. John said that during his last session when I had asked him why he "could not disagree" with me, he had felt that I was reprimanding him for being angry. I asked him again why he had not been able to stay and "disagree" with me. He then became aware that he had run out of my office because he feared the wrath of his internalized mother that he had projected onto me. He said that he had always found it difficult to disagree with people and noted that he had "complained" to me about his wife instead of complaining to her directly. John said that he had run away from his wife, his colleagues, and me, because he feared that he might lose his temper and become physically violent. He remembered having similar fears when he played competitive sports. John then decided that he needed to stop running away from me when he was angry, so that he could learn how to control his anger. He then wondered whether he provoked people because, unconsciously, he wanted to be put down and controlled, and he thought of the nursery rhyme, "Georgie Porgy Puddin' Pie, kissed the girls and made them cry. When the boys came out to play, Georgie Porgy ran away." He realized that he had thought of this rhyme because it meant that if he had been aggressive toward his mother, his father would have come out against him.

As I continued to confront John more directly, he became less frightened of his anger at me for doing so. He, therefore, ceased running out of our sessions and became more assertive with me. He began breaking my rules by coming late to his sessions. I pointed this out, and he told me that his mother was often late when meeting him. John now realized that being late was hostile, and that he was doing to me what his mother had done to him. In one session, John refused to lie down on the couch. I told him that he was breaking my rule, and he then laid down. He said he was pleased both that I insisted that he lay down, and that I did not reject him by withdrawing from him like his mother would have done. He said that when I told him to lie down on the couch, he knew that I cared. Angrily, he added, "My mother didn't give a shit about me." John then said that although he often argued with me, on weekends he felt lost without me because I had become very important to him. This thought reminded him of his frightening early thoughts that his mother had been "mutilated." He next recalled how his grandmother had hovered over him with the slivers of soap. He associated that his wife was in no way like his mother or grandmother, and then—for the first time—he spoke freely about making love to his wife. Tearfully, he then said that he felt that women disliked men. I told him that most women liked men, but that he had trouble accepting this because apparently his mother had not liked men. As John left this session, he smiled and said that I was the first person who cared enough to set limits on him and argue rationally with him.

As John gradually learned how to be appropriately aggressive with me, he realized that he had not been able to set suitable limits on his children because his father had not been there to do so for him. He then began to set appropriate limits on his children, and he was pleased.

A month later John came to understand that to avoid having erotic feelings with women whom he thought of as mother figures he had convinced himself that his wife and I were unattractive. He again noted that neither his wife nor I had deserved his hostility, which he now knew belonged to his mother. This new insight allowed him to have warm, comfortable feelings toward both his wife and me, and increased his desire to get physically close to us.

John now realized that he had chosen his wife because she had aggressive, masculine qualities. Choosing a wife with masculine qualities allowed him to unconsciously fantasy that she had a penis, and that, therefore, she would not be envious of his penis and want to take it from him—like his mother and grandmother had taken his feces. He had feared that a feminine wife would have been envious of his penis—like he felt his mother must have been.

John began to understand that when he put on women's clothing and looked in the mirror, he was seeing himself "as a woman with a penis." Then John, who had always called me "Dr. Loeb," had a slip of the tongue and called me "Mrs. Loeb." He recognized his slip and jokingly said that his slip devalued me because he thought the psychoanalysis was a waste of time. I suggested that his slip took away the penis that he had just given me. Insightfully, he laughed and said that he damned me if I had a penis and damned me if I did not. He elaborated on these thoughts and said that he both resented my setting limits on him and my not setting limits on him. He said that when I was silent and passive, he saw me as weak, ineffectual, envious, and wimpy, but that when I set limits on him, he saw me as powerful, controlling, intrusive, and masculine. John then said that when he saw me as weak and lacking a penis, he would become anxious. He said he was pleased that I set limits on him and did not let him get away with things. John added that, when he was a child, his not having limits frightened him.

For the first time, John was able to let his wife know that he wanted to play with her anus. His interest in her anus, he thought, was because his mother and grandmother put slivers of soap up his anus. His wife was pleased and receptive to his proposal, and he was relieved. Unlike his wife, his mother had never cared what he wanted to do—she just wanted him to do what she told him to do.

John was pleased because he was feeling "less hostile" toward himself, me, his wife, and his colleagues. He continued, however, to banter with and insult me. Once again, John sat up and refused to lie down. He remained on the couch, but this time with his back toward me. He was amazed that he could love and hate the same person at the same time. He then remembered that he had similar ambivalent feelings toward his mother. John again noted that my smile was unlike his mother's, which, he felt was a facade to cover up her hatefulness. He said that he did not want to think about ending the psychoanalysis and separating from me. John recalled how bad he had felt when his mother had avoided him by staying in her third floor bedroom. He feared that he would feel the same way when the psychoanalysis ended. He now clearly understood that when his mother left him and went to her bedroom, he had taken her in [identified with the lost object] to diminish his separation anxiety. This session, when I told him that our time was up, he accused me of rejecting him. I repeated that our time was up, and he said that he was pleased with the limits I was setting on him. He said that his mother had not been concerned when she separated from him, but he had trouble separating himself from her. John began wondering whether my concern for him would make it easier for him to separate from me.

In our next session, John reported the following dream: *He was sexually aroused, and jealous of other people who were close and inter-*

ested in each other. He then lay down on my couch, and my face was over him. I then reached over and held his hands. He associated to the dream that yesterday his wife had put her arms around him and told him that she felt that they had become closer and more emotionally dependent upon each other. John said that she had looked very good to him, and he had agreed that they had become more emotionally dependent upon each other. John felt good that he was now able to feel this way without feeling like he was a "bad little boy." He said, with strong emotion, that his mother was a "real castrator," and that she had not allowed him to be "aggressive or masculine." John said that he now had learned that he could be both aggressive and masculine, and still be accepted by both his wife and me. John suspected that his mother and grandmother had wanted him to act like a little girl, but he now knew that both his wife and I wanted him to act like a grown man. This dream, John said, differed from his earlier dream in which I had reached over and grabbed his hands to prevent him from hitting me. In this dream, he said, I held his hands "lovingly."

John said he was pleased that he had me to help him, but he was sorry that he could not take me with him to the beach. He said that although, occasionally, he still verbally attacked me, he was very pleased that he was no longer afraid of being dependent on either myself or his wife. He added that he and his wife were no longer talking about getting a divorce.

Several weeks later, John told me that he liked my dress and wanted to touch it, put it on, and identify himself as a woman. He then remembered that he had once touched his penis to his mother's hair while she was sleeping, and that the first time he masturbated it was with his mother's Kotex pad. The night after this session, he **dreamed** that *he went up to his mother and touched her paisley dress.* John **associated** that the intimacy of the analysis was "at odds with his not having a physical sexual relationship with me." He fantasied coming up to me, putting his arms around me, and holding me. He wanted me to hold him with his face on my hair. He interjected that his father had been embarrassed about sex and had given John the impression that women did not enjoy it. Both parents had conveyed to him that it was improper for them to show interest in each other in public places.

When I resumed our sessions after I returned from being away, John said he was pleased to see me. Tearfully, he said he had felt lonely when I was away. John said, "I'm painfully reenacting my childhood in my psychoanalysis, and I'm very grateful to have this opportunity. You mean more to me than any other woman." He said that he was pleased that, unlike his mother, I never put him down by telling him that he was bad or that I did not like him. John said that while I was away, his mother had put him down and made him feel inadequate by calling his new, very expensive sports car a "cute little car." He said that now, when his wife disagreed with him, he no longer put his mother onto her and felt that she was being nasty. This change made him feel good about himself. He added, however, that sometimes he still felt put down—even when no one was putting him down. John was now very aware that at times he had difficulty differentiating other people from his mother, and that at times he discharged his angry feelings, which belonged to his mother, onto others. If the others retaliated, he then felt justified. He explained that he was now consciously aware that he had been attracted to women that put him down because, when they did so, he unconsciously felt justified in his having been angry toward his mother.

During one session I was ill, and I looked it. He worried that I would be too sick to be able to see him the next day. The next day he came for his appointment and told me that immediately after leaving my office yesterday, he had impulsively gone home, put on his wife's underclothing, and masturbated. I gave him the following interpretation:

Unconsciously, he might have feared that I would die of my illness and that he would lose me. To prevent, or compensate for, such a loss, perhaps he had put on clothing resembling mine and pretended that he was me.

He readily agreed with my interpretation, and was startled when he remembered that it was just after his grandmother fell ill and died that he first cross-dressed. John then told me that he had mixed feelings when his grandmother died. She had not been a well-dressed, perfumed, attractive woman like his mother. Instead, she "always wore an apron and was down to earth." John said that he had loved her. Although his mother had expected him to be perfect and well mannered, "like a little girl who just stepped out of a bandbox," his grandmother did not expect that from him—she only expected him to be clean. He said that he regretted that he had not told her that he loved her before she died. With embarrassment, he described to me how, when she died, he had put on her apron and had masturbated. He next told me that when he saw his mother's caesarian section scar and her red vulva, he had the thought that she had been castrated. I further interpreted that his free associations had linked my illness and possible death to his grandmother's death and to his mother's lack of a penis. I told him that he restored my health, his grandmother's life, and his mother's penis, by impulsively putting on women's clothing and seeing his penis in women's clothing. In this way, he was unconsciously, symbolically restoring my health, his grandmother's life, and his mother's penis.

He responded that, when I looked ill, he must have unconsciously thought that I was castrated, so he had put on women's clothing to give me the penis that he unconsciously thought I had lost. He had put on women's clothing and had pretended that he was me with a penis. John then remembered that, as a young boy, he had fantasied giving his mother a penis so that she would not want to remove his penis—like she had removed his feces. John then associated that when he had seen his mother's scar and vulva in the bathtub, he must have worried that he too might have his penis cut off. He felt that although his mother did not value either himself or his father as males, she must have envied their having penises. John then again remembered that when he saw his mother standing naked in the bathtub, he had the thought that her penis had been cut off. He said that he must have then feared that his penis could also be cut off.

That night John dreamed that *he was touching me.* He associated that he could not remember whether, when he was a young boy, he had touched his mother's hair with his penis or had just fantasied that he had done so. John next remembered the movie *The Devil and Miss Jones.* He said that in this movie there was a mutilated woman in a bathtub, and that he could not look at her. John said that he did not want to see the woman in the movie, or think of me as castrated. Instead, he wanted to see me as Abraham Lincoln—that is, perfect, but not loveable. It frightened him to think that he might be stronger than either his mother, his wife, or me.

John said that although his mother vigorously protested against anything sexual, she was "altogether too seductive with her tight clothing and soft, breathy voice." Growing up, he had fantasied that he could overcome his mother's anger at men by being sexual with her. He recalled that sometimes he could manipulate his mother. John then said that, because I was not saying anything, he felt that I was putting him down for having sexual desires. He said that he worried that I could read his mind and learn that he now wanted to put on women's clothing.

Returning from a ten-day trip, John again said that my smile looked sweet and not like his mother's insincere smile. He said that because of his psychoanalysis, he was now able to take care of himself the way his mother should have taken care of him. As a child he had viewed himself as a pathetic, weak person, who had not been able to take care of himself, and that, therefore, he had permitted his mother to put him down. John said that this thought made him feel guilty. He said that he had sent his mother a Mother's Day card, but felt no guilt for wanting, instead, to give her a "kick in the ass." John mentioned that his mother was still attractive at 65. He said that making love to me would violate our relationship—just like it would have violated his relationship with his mother. He wanted to feel I was invested in "him" and not just in his "psychoanalysis." He then fantasied that a car hit me and that he had to find a new psychoanalyst. John remembered that in adolescence he had frequently behaved badly to try to get his mother's attention and concern. He then recognized he had insulted me to get my attention so that I would meet his needs.

After we worked through his guilt over his having responded sexually to his seductive mother, he stopped feeling defective for being sexually aroused by her. He was then able to accept his sexual attraction to his mother and still remain close to her. Once John no longer felt conflicted over his dependent and sexual feelings for his mother, he could tolerate her behavior better. He then no longer feared that he would be castrated for wanting to be close to a woman. Now that John understood the origin of his castration anxiety, he no longer felt it so intensely, and no longer needed to put on women's clothing to unconsciously prove to himself that women were not castrated.

John realized that he had distanced himself from his mother and felt guilty for doing so because his mother had given him more than many of his friends got. He also realized that he experienced guilt when he outdid other men, because he fantasied that if he did so, his mother would like him better. Once he understood this, he was able to compete successfully without feeling guilt.

A few sessions later, I was again wearing dance tights with seams down the back. He said that they aroused him sexually, which made him feel guilty—like he had been when he saw his mother straighten the seams in her stockings.

John dreamed that *I told him that he was ready to finish his analysis*. He associated that his present project at work was almost completed, and within a year he would need to begin a new project in a distant city. Therefore, we discussed a termination date and planned to finish in about a year. He said that this made him feel both sad and angry. John said that although he had learned a great deal in his analysis, he felt that he had become too dependent upon me—like he had been too dependent upon his mother. John then associated to his anger with his controlling mother for intrusively putting slivers of Ivory soap up his rectum every morning. He now realized that he had withheld his feces to retaliate against his mother and maintain his independence from her. This same anger, later led him to also withhold his feelings and thoughts from her. Subsequently, he had acted out this withholding behavior with others—especially with women with whom he was close. Although before his analysis, he could not talk freely to anyone—not even his wife—he could now talk freely to many people. John said that he knew that he would never be able to talk freely with his mother.

In spite of all the insight that John had acquired during his four-year psychoanalysis, he realized that he had not learned everything. He said that, just like cleaning out his rectum every day was futile for his mother and grandmother because more feces were always coming along, finishing analysis was also futile because more thoughts would always come along. He felt that my telling him to free associate was like his mother telling him to "just let loose and freely let the feces out." John said that he wanted to finish his analysis, but that he did not want to leave me.

John dreamed that *he was riding a horse down a road, and a dog threatened to bite his horse. He grabbed the dog by its canine teeth and hurled it over his head. The dog came back, and John feared that the dog would cut his finger, but it did not.* John associated that he should have had a weapon in the dream to protect him from the dog. He then recalled a formerly repressed memory: He told me that his mother had always kept a knife in the bathroom to **cut** off the pieces of Ivory soap she put up his rectum. The knife had been there when he put the propeller of his toy airplane into his penis, and his grandmother told him that "*she or his mother would have to cut it off.*" He then realized that this experience, combined with the following other experiences, had led to his intense fear of castration: (1) His grandmother had told him that *if he played with his penis, it would fall off.* (2) He had seen that his naked *mother* in the bathtub *lacked a penis.* (3) His mother and grandmother had told him *not to make noise when he urinated*, and his mother had told him to *sit down to urinate.* (4) His mother had told him that she spit on his hair *to make* *every hair stay in place because nothing on little boys should be allowed to stick out.* (5) His mother had told him to urinate out the car door and then told him *that his stream was too high and went too far.* (6) His mother and grandmother had often told him, *"Don't get too big for your britches."* (7) His mother and his grandmother had consistently shown *hostility toward men.*

That night John dreamed that *he was passive with three women.* He associated that his wife often complained that he was too passive during sex. Defensively, he told me that if he had been totally passive, they would never have had sex. He added that when his mother paraded around nude, it was better for him to be passive than for him to respond to her seductiveness.

Two months later John dreamed that *he was driving a little car, and then he was riding a bicycle.* Associating to the dream, he recalled that his mother had put him down for spending too much on cars, and that his wife complained that he did not give her enough money. Money, he said, was power, and he did not want to give power to others. He recognized that he had identified with his mother's self-centeredness, selfishness, inflexibility, and rigidity. Because of this, his wife and children had been "short changed." He recognized that by not giving money to his wife and children, he had been punishing them for what his mother had done to him. He wanted to become more flexible, but he realized that, when he tried to loosen up, he came into conflict with his internalized, rigid mother. These insights permitted John to give his wife and children more money, show them more affection, and have more fun with them.

At one point, John became anxious and wanted to stop his psycho-analysis immediately. From his associations, we learned that his thoughts of stopping were because he felt guilty for doing better with his family than his father had done with his. He said that he also wanted to stop because he irrationally feared that he would take me away from my husband. He then realized that he had felt responsible for driving his father away from his mother. John then reassured himself by remembering that he had not completely won his mother for himself because his mother had chosen to move in with her own parents. John felt good after arriving at these insights, and he decided that he was going to accept his success in the psychoanalysis and complete it.

A week later, John's mother sent him a birthday card with a long poem she had written that documented all the bad things that he had done while growing up. He said that, although she had her limitations, she was not all bad, and had softened with age. He summed up by saying that because he had not wished to lose his mother, he had "taken her in—for better or worse—mostly for worse." He added that now, faced with termination, he did not want to lose me and was "taking me in—for better or worse—mostly for better."

John said that although his analysis had been difficult, it had helped him a great deal. He was pleased with his accomplishment, but felt a great sense of impending loss. John said that he wanted to hang on to me—like he had wanted to hang on to his mother. However, he added, his mother was always very hostile toward him, whereas I never was. He remembered that he had wrongly accused me of criticizing him, when actually he was projecting his mother's criticisms of him onto me. He said that his mother never praised him without simultaneously putting him down. She would say things like, "You are wonderful, but you were late for supper," or "It is great that you got high grades, but your room is a mess." He remembered that although his grandmother's house was always neat, organized, and easy to live in, it was an unhappy place.

John felt ashamed and guilty that he had abused women in the past. He knew now that he had abused them because of the anger that he had felt toward his mother. He said he no longer had any impulse to abuse women, and what was most important to him was that, because of the psychoanalysis, he was now able to like himself. He said, "I have changed over the last four years. I'm not the same person. I have become less controlling, and I no longer have to deride or argue with my wife or you to keep you both at a distance. This is because I no longer fear that you or my wife has power and authority over me like my mother did. When I'm very tense, however, I'm still tempted to put on women's clothing—but I'm not compelled to do so, and I don't. Since I no longer fear becoming dependent on and controlled by my wife or you, I can now communicate with you both without difficulty." He felt, however, that he could now continue the psychoanalytic process by himself because, just as he no longer had to withhold his feces, he no longer had to withhold his thoughts.

CONCLUSIONS

John's father permanently abandoned him when he was four, and his mother frequently withdrew from him by secluding herself in her bedroom. When his mother left him he would tearfully ask his grandmother,

"When is mommy coming back to Monkey?" A knife was kept in the bathroom and used to *take off* pieces of soap to put into his anus to *remove* his feces. When he was about 5-years-old, he saw his mother in the bathtub and saw that she lacked a penis. He assumed that her penis had been *taken off* like the slivers of soap had been *taken off* and used to *take off* his feces. This led him to fear that he could lose his penis like, he assumed, his mother had lost hers. The following subsequent events had accentuated this fear:

1. His grandmother had disapprovingly told him "if you play with your penis, it will fall off."
2. His grandmother had found him putting the propeller of his toy airplane into the meatus of his penis and disapprovingly told him that "it would have to be *cut out*." He thought she meant that "his penis would have to be *cut off*."
3. His mother and grandmother had both told him to "sit down and don't make noise when you urinate."
4. His mother would spit on his hair to make every hair stay in place, and told him that "nothing on little boys should be allowed to stick out."
5. On a trip, his mother told him to urinate out the car door and then told him, "Your stream is too high and goes too far."
6. His mother and grandmother had often told him, "Don't get too big for your britches." He had interpreted this to mean, "Don't get an erection."
7. His mother and his grandmother were consistently spiteful toward his father, his grandfather, and all other men.

Thus, as a small child, John had multiple experiences that led him unconsciously to fear that if he allowed himself to be aggressive, masculine, and enjoy his penis, (1) he might be castrated and/or (2) he might be abandoned by his mother and his grandmother—just like he had been abandoned by his father.

Then, in puberty, two events occurred that exaggerated these two unconscious fears. First, he experienced a pubescent increase in his sexual drive, which intensified his fear of castration. And, second, he experienced his grandmother's death, which intensified his fear of abandonment. To calm his anxiety over these two unconscious fears, he developed his symptom of cross-dressing while looking at himself in a mirror.

This symptom reduced his *castration anxiety* by demonstrating to him that women were not castrated because, like him, they had penises hidden underneath their clothing. Also, this symptom reduced his *separation anxiety* by his identification with the potentially lost objects—his mother and grandmother. Once John became consciously aware of both his castration anxiety and his separation anxiety and how these two anxieties began, his cross-dressing ceased.

FOLLOW UP

John contacted me for two consecutive years following termination. He told me that he was not cross-dressing and was continuing to do well both at work and with his wife and children. Twenty years after his psychoanalysis ended, I called him and learned that his wife was pleased with him and that his cross-dressing had not resumed. He sent me a letter saying that he was still free-associating and wished he could still discuss his dreams with me.

THE PSYCHOANALYTIC RESOLUTION OF
TRANSVESTITE SYMPTOMS IN A MAN

This chapter describes Paul's successful psychoanalysis. His initial evaluation took ten sessions because he did not want to tell me of his cross-dressing at first. Paul's initial mother and father-transference resistances had to be dealt with next. After that, I will present chronologically the formerly repressed and/or isolated memories that Paul remembered or reconnected during his psychoanalysis. Next, I describe how Paul's father-transference was worked through, how Paul's mother fostered his illness, and the predominant defenses that Paul used as resistances during the analysis. I will then summarize Paul's final year of psychoanalysis and his termination phase. Finally, I will present the genetic-dynamic understanding that Paul attained during his psychoanalysis, and how this resulted in the elimination of his symptom of cross-dressing.

INITIAL EVALUATION

Paul was a thirty-six-year-old disheveled, married, physicist. He had two sons, ages 4 and 10. When Paul's four-year-old, adopted son said that he was a girl in a boy's body and asked to have his penis cut off, Paul began to worry that he had somehow inadvertently transmitted his own sexual problem onto his son. So he sought psychoanalytic therapy for both his son and himself. Although, unlike his son, Paul had never felt he was a woman in a man's body, he felt deviant and ashamed because, since he began masturbating in puberty, he had always felt compelled to do so while wearing women's underclothing and looking at himself in a mirror. He said that he had never before told anyone of this. Before he got married, this had been his only sexual outlet and it remained his chief sexual outlet after marriage. He rarely attempted intercourse with his wife, and when he did, he became anxious and often impotent.

Beginning when he was five years old, whenever Paul saw a representation of a female person—that is a dummy, puppet, robot, manikin, or doll, he became both fascinated and terrified. Thereafter, whenever he saw a real woman or girl, he had to scrutinize her to determine whether she was real or fake. He believed that fake female persons were perfect, but that real ones were not. This was an obsessive symptom. He was neither psychotic nor phobic (Rangell 1952). At age nine, Paul began building robots. Because he knew for certain that they were not real, these robots did not frighten him, nor did he obsess about them. Besides obsessing about fake representations of women he also obsessed about whether he was working enough or exercising enough. At times these obsessional thoughts kept him awake at night. He said that, like his mother, he kept everything "organized, neat, and clean."

During puberty Paul began having wet dreams in which he always was wearing women's sexy underclothing. When he then began to masturbate, he always either wore or fantasied that he was wearing provocative women's underclothing. At this time whenever he saw an attractively dressed woman he became anxious and would begin to obsess and ponder over whether she was a real woman or a fake. Occasionally, while so obsessing, he became sexually aroused.

Paul was an only child. His father, 62, was a scientist of Norwegian descent and was away at war until Paul was four. When his father returned, his father's leg wound made it difficult for him to walk. Paul could not remember which leg had been damaged. Paul's father then worked away from home for months at a time. Paul described his father as "passive, even-tempered, distant, and unaffectionate." Paul felt bad that his father was crippled and passive. Paul's father almost never reprimanded or disciplined Paul. Paul remembered seeing his father angry only three times: (1) Paul's father bought Paul a model airplane, but would not let Paul help him put it together. This angered Paul, so Paul smashed the airplane. Paul's father shook with fury, but said nothing, and left the room quietly. (2) At age seven, Paul stubbornly refused to do something his father had asked him to do. Paul's father became enraged, and "limping pathetically" came after Paul "menacingly." Paul fled—easily outrunning his crippled father. When, several hours later, Paul returned home, his father passively and quietly ignored Paul. (3) Once, when Paul had been rude to his mother, his father—showing visible exasperation—silently and gently grabbed Paul's arm.

During high school, Paul's father supplied Paul with materials so that Paul could complete complex scientific projects on his own. Paul loved his father for this and, like him, became a scientist.

Paul's mother, 61, was "an outgoing, intelligent, attractive, dark-skinned brunette of Irish extraction." She exercised to stay in shape and spent a great deal of time and money on cosmetics and clothing. She was an "extremely tidy homemaker," and often criticized Paul for being "messy." "Her father had spoiled her," and she controlled Paul's father by "pretending to be helpless and dependent." When Paul's father was away, she became very competent and self-sufficient. She frequently told Paul that he could accomplish anything he wished. However, when he succeeded at some task, she would either ignore his accomplishment or tell him that he could have done better. During his teens, Paul continually quarreled with his mother. His father stayed out of these arguments.

Paul felt guilty because both of his parents let him get away with things and gave him almost everything he wanted.

Paul's grades in high school were mediocre, but he built a robot that won first prize in the State Science Fair. He felt guilty that his friend had not won, so he helped his friend win first prize the following year. His SAT scores were extremely high, and in college, he got top grades with little effort. After achieving a Ph.D., he became an assistant professor at a prestigious university. Although his research was excellent, he was blocked from writing papers, so he took a job with a major corporation. There, he did not assert himself, allowed others to take credit for his work, and was never promoted. He sought praise, but when he received it, he felt unworthy of it.

Paul's tonsils were removed when he was three. As an adult, he often "overdid it" and injured himself when he exercised. He occasionally suffered from prostatitis.

Paul recalled that for nine months during his thirteenth year he and his mother had moved 200 miles away from his father so that Paul could attend a special school. There, he and his mother lived in a three-room apartment. They shared a bedroom, but had separate beds. Paul missed his father and began to argue frequently with his mother. The few times that Paul's father visited them on weekends, Paul would continue to share the bedroom with his mother, while his father slept on the couch in the living room. This arrangement made Paul feel guilty and awkward.

After Paul and his mother returned to live with his father, Paul began having romantic fantasies about various girls in his school, who, unlike his mother, were fair-skinned, blue-eyed, and blond. He said that he "idealized" these girls and worked out to make his body "as perfect as theirs."[1] He would fantasy that he was wearing their underclothing, when he put on his mother's underwear to masturbate.

Paul remembered that when he was fifteen, a girlfriend asked him to have intercourse with her, he became frightened and impotent.

In college, Paul began dating his future wife, Jane. She was fair-skinned, blue-eyed, and blond. He idealized her, and masturbated while fantasying that he was wearing her underclothing. After dating her for several months, she tried to initiate intercourse with him. Each time she tried, he became anxious and impotent. Finally, after he turned off the lights, he completed the act. After their marriage, whenever Paul saw Jane in her underclothing, he would become disgusted, his testicles would retract, and he would become impotent. Afterward, however, he would put on her underclothing, look at himself in the mirror, and successfully masturbate to orgasm. After several months of marriage, when he put on his wife's underclothing to masturbate, he could no longer become aroused by thinking of Jane. He had to think of some other blued-eyed, blond woman to get aroused.

Because of these painful problems, Paul started in psychoanalysis four-times-a-week.

INITIAL MOTHER-TRANSFERENCE RESISTANCE

Paul did not tell me of his cross-dressing until his tenth visit. After telling me, he fell silent. I pointed out his silence, and he said that he feared that I would criticize him for cross-dressing like his mother would have. After becoming aware of this mother-transference, he was able to freely associate.

INITIAL FATHER-TRANSFERENCE RESISTANCE

During the first three months of the analysis my abstinence, lack of criticism, passivity, and silence reminded Paul of his reserved, passive, distant, and silent father. This led Paul to transfer the positive feelings he had toward his father onto me. I did not interfere with this positive transference, and this resulted in a strong therapeutic alliance that lasted for

---

[1]Much later in the psychoanalysis he realized that by "idealizing" them and making his body "as perfect as theirs," he was unconsciously giving them penises to deny their castration.

over two-and-one-half-years. This strong therapeutic alliance together with Paul's intense shame over his cross-dressing motivated him to work hard in his psychoanalysis. During this period, Paul repeatedly told me of the time he had become angry and smashed his model airplane because his father had assembled it and had not let Paul do it. Paul also reported several incidents at work in which he had asked his supervisors for assistance, and then had become angry with them when they helped him. When Paul attempted to act out this pattern of behavior with me in the transference, I interpreted his repetition compulsion. This further enhanced our therapeutic alliance and freed Paul up so that he could self-analyze. I made interpretations only when his resistances overwhelmed him.

REPRESSED CHILDHOOD MEMORIES RECOVERED DURING THE FIRST FIVE YEARS OF PAUL'S PSYCHOANALYSIS

Memories from His Third Year

Paul recalled that he took a lawn mower apart, stuck hair pins into electric outlets to watch the sparks fly, and turned-off an escalator in a department store. In each of these instances, his mother admonished him gently while displaying pride in his accomplishments. This approval encouraged him to believe that he had powerful, magical abilities. Paul also remembered seeing female genitalia while watching his mother change a baby girl's diapers.

Memories from His Fourth Year

(1) Paul remembered that he would hit the pillows on the couch when his mother left him with a baby sitter. Eventually, Paul realized that he had done this because he was angry with his mother for leaving him. He then recalled becoming angry when his mother reprimanded him for coming home from college unexpectedly and interrupting a party she was having. Eventually, he realized that this was why he became disproportionately angry when either his wife, Jane, or his secretary was not immediately available. Much later in his psychoanalysis he realized that such anger at his wife dissipated after they had intercourse. He also realized that, at times, he started arguments with Jane to push her away like he had started arguments with his mother to push her away.

(2) Paul also remembered jumping, lightheartedly, on his father's back to play "horsey." His father screamed in pain. Paul feared that he had further damaged his already crippled father. However, Paul's action

permanently cured his father's chronic back pain. This experience again enhanced Paul's belief that he had special magical power.

Memories from his Fifth Year

(1) When Paul was about four and one-half, his mother resized his father's army uniform to fit Paul. Paul began to wear it proudly every day until a playmate accused him of "impersonating an officer." After that, Paul refused to put on the uniform again. Later in his psychoanalysis he realized that he had abruptly stopped wearing the uniform because he had feared his unconscious, omnipotent-magical wish to supplant his father.

(2) During church services Paul was playing with his penis while looking at his "dressed-up" mother. Quietly, but angrily, she told him to stop. He refused.

(3) In school, a classmate's ring got stuck on her finger. Her finger turned blue. The teacher said, "We must cut it off." Paul became terrified. He thought the teacher meant that she was going to "cut off" her finger. While telling me of this episode, Paul made a slip of the tongue and said, "her finger was cut off," when he meant to say "her ring was cut off."

(4) He saw a classmate get run over and killed by a car. Later he would fantasy that he was a doctor putting her mutilated body back together.

(5) He watched his mother change a little girl's diaper. He again told me that this was the "first time he saw that a girl lacked a penis."[2] Several days after that, he became terrified when he watched his mother put on, and then take off, a hand puppet. He could never understand why he had become so extremely upset when he witnessed this apparently innocuous incident. It was immediately after these two experiences that his obsessive fear of, and fascination with, puppets, robots, manikins, dummies, dolls, men wearing women's clothing, and persons with physical disabilities began.[3]

---

[2]Paul had seen—and repressed that he had seen—female genitalia when he was three-, six-, and eight-years-old. He also remembered that when he was eleven, he "did not know what female genitalia looked like," "knew nothing about sexual intercourse," and believed that "women's genitalia were the same as men's." Because he had originally repressed each of these experiences, when he remembered only one of them, he described it as the first time he had seen that a female lacked a penis.

[3]When Paul began psychoanalysis, he was aware that he was both fascinated and frightened by simulated humans. It was much later, in his psychoanalysis that he became aware that he had also always been, frightened and fascinated by men wearing women's clothing and persons with physical disabilities.

Memories from His Sixth Year

Paul saw the movie, *Pinocchio*. When the puppet maker threatened to splinter Pinocchio, Paul had become terrified. That night, Paul **dreamed** that *a big giant was chasing him and was going to smash him.* He awoke frightened, got into his parents' bed, and slept between them.

Memories from His Seventh Year

1.) He had stopped masturbating in Church.

2.) He saw a picture of a man and a woman copulating and felt disgusted by the woman's genitalia.

3.) He began to put himself down and to feel inadequate.

4.) He repeatedly fantasied that he would disguise himself as a woman to prevent dangerous robbers from harming him.[4]

REPRESSED MEMORIES RECOVERED DURING THE SIXTH YEAR OF PAUL'S PSYCHOANALYSIS

Suddenly, Paul developed a new compulsion. When obsessing whether a woman was a real person or simulated person, he became compelled to "search for a seam in her neck." This compulsion seemed ridiculous to him, but he was unable to stop doing it. Several months after this compulsive behavior began, while searching for a seam in a woman's neck, he suddenly remembered that when he was five years old, and he saw the little girl's genital area, he had hypothesized that he was looking at a little boy who was wearing a "tight fitting girl-suit costume." He had then further hypothesized that the suit "must have had a seam through which the little boy had entered."

Months later, through his psychoanalysis, Paul understood that he had invented this girl-costume hypothesis to defend against the castration anxiety he had experienced when he saw that the little girl lacked a penis—that is, he had hypothesized that the little baby actually had a penis hidden within her girl-costume.

---

[4]Toward the end of his analysis, while thinking about this memory, Paul realized that he had worn women's underclothing, not only to achieve sexual gratification and deny their castration, but also to hide and protect his penis from "dangerous robbers" who might want to take it.

REPRESSED MEMORIES RECOVERED DURING THE
EIGHTH YEAR OF PAUL'S PSYCHOANALYSIS

While wondering where his inhibitory guilt came from, he remembered the following two significant events from his fifth year:

(1) His parents had installed a new, white, living room carpet, and they told him never to eat or drink on it. He disobeyed and spilled grape juice on it. His mother became furious and called his father home from work. When his father arrived, he remained calm and neither reprimanded nor punished Paul. Paul was disappointed that his father did not show anger or discipline him. I pointed out to Paul that his overly-permissive, non-limit-setting, parents had enjoyed and unintentionally encouraged his creative misbehavior instead of setting appropriate external limits on him. I also suggested that he might have developed his excessively punitive, inhibitory internal conscience to control what he felt to be his externally-unrestricted power.

(2) Paul then recalled that when his mother had praised him and told him that he could accomplish anything that he desired, he had felt that she was telling him that all he had to do was make a wish and it would come true. This had frightened Paul and led him to worry that his angry, destructive wishes toward his calm, passive, quiet, disabled father might come true because his father seemed so weak and ineffectual. Paul then realized that he had developed his internal, inhibitory guilt to prevent what he believed to be his omnipotent magical wish-power from harming his father.

Soon after Paul realized that, as a child, he had imposed excessive internal controls on himself, to control what he believed to be his powerful, magical wish-power; he remembered a second very significant event that also occurred when he was five:

He was playing with a balloon-on-a-stick in a grocery store. He saw Coca-Cola bottles stacked in a display. Fancifully, he had the wish that he could magically knock down the stack of Coca-Cola bottles by waving his balloon-on-a-stick toward it. Playfully, he did so, and, to his amazement, the bottles tumbled down around him breaking on the floor. Because his balloon had not touched the bottles, he became convinced that his playful wish had worked magic. Therefore, although no one blamed or punished him for causing the bottles to fall, he felt responsible and guilty. Paul said, "Although no one punished me, I punished myself magically by fearing that some broken glass had cut me or gotten into my eyes. It's funny, right now I'm rubbing my eyes as though I had glass in them. Since then, I have feared that if I succeed at something, something bad will happen to me." Paul added, "I think I was holding my penis when the Coca-Cola bottles exploded." I pointed out his defensive doubting, by repeating his word, "think?" He replied, "I know I was playing with myself at the time."

Soon after remembering this, Paul remembered that, when he was thirteen, while sharing the bedroom with his mother, he had once seen her vaginal area and had become disgusted. Several days after seeing her genitals, his mother's skirt rode up as she got out of her car, and he saw her stockings, garter belt, and sheer see-through under panties. That evening he put on her stockings, garter belt, and under panties, looked at himself in the mirror, and masturbated. This was the first time he cross-dressed and the first time he had an orgasm. Paul said this was his "most erotic experience." His mother then went away for several weeks, and he stayed with a friend. While she was away, he became curious about girls his own age, and he masturbated thinking of them without wearing his mother's underclothing. When his mother returned, he resumed his cross-dressing.

Paul now also remembered that when he was a small boy his mother would change her menstrual pads in front of him without explaining why she was bleeding. When he saw her blood, he became disgusted and extremely frightened. He also recalled that before his father had returned from the war, his mother had undressed in front of him and had slept with him. Even during his puberty his mother had twice come out of the shower naked in front of him. Then, while looking at home movies of his childhood, Paul observed that his mother was always wearing very low-cut blouses and extremely short skirts. Paul now said that beginning in puberty, whenever he thought of his mother he had become impotent. He now also observed that he had always avoided girls that resembled his mother. The following week when his wife put a bedspread on their bed that his parents had used, it triggered a memory of his mother and he became impotent and cried.

Paul recognized that *part* of the excessive irrational anger that he had felt toward Jane was because she was *not* his mother. He then experienced "unreasonable sadness" because, now that he had achieved his vocational quest, he was still unable to win his mother. This, for him, was a mid-life crisis.

Now, Paul understood why he always had to turn off the lights to consummate intercourse with his wife. He did so both to avoid seeing what he felt to be his wife's "dirty, imperfect, and disgusting" genitals and to more easily fantasy that he was wearing women's underclothing. After Paul became aware of his castration anxiety and its origin, he became able to leave the lights on when he had intercourse. He could now look at Jane's genitals without becoming anxious or impotent.

WORKING THROUGH PAUL'S FATHER-TRANSFERENCE

At times, Paul had become angry with me without knowing why. In his 347th session he noted that this anger occurred whenever either he or I canceled a session. Three months later, he became angry with me after telling me that, while recklessly racing to pass another car, he had skidded his high-speed sports car into a ditch. Again he said he did not know why he became so angry. I asked if he might be angry with me because I had not responded when he told me of his accident. Angrily, he replied that, if I really cared about him, I would have rebuked him for driving recklessly. I asked him if my silence and passivity made him feel that I was as remote from—and indifferent toward—him as his passive, silent father had seemed to be. Paul replied, "yes," and recalled that when he was an adolescent, his father had bought him both a motorcycle and a very fast car. These gifts had made him feel that his father did not care about Paul's safety. Over the next few sessions, Paul reminisced about other instances in which he had been angry with his father for being passive, remote, and silent and, therefore, seemingly indifferent and uncaring:

(1) Paul's father had never praised him for getting top grades in school.

(2) His father had bought him gifts but did not spend time with him.

(3) During early adolescence, Paul's mother told him that his father observed that Paul was not dating and wondered if Paul were homosexual. Paul became angry that his father did not ask him directly about this.

(4) When Jane went into labor, Paul exuberantly told his father, but his father said that revealing such emotions was effeminate.

(5) Paul especially resented that his father had not angrily objected to Paul's sharing a bedroom with his mother.

Paul wondered if his father concealed his anger by becoming passive, silent, and aloof. Paul then realized that his father's failure to express anger and thereby set a limit on Paul's aggression, had led Paul to believe that he could easily overpower his father and take his father's place with his mother. This had caused Paul to feel guilty if he did anything that made him believe that he had successfully outdone or surpassed his pathetically hobbled father. Paul then realized that, because of this guilt, he had repressed—and, thereafter, always inhibited—his own aggressive and sexual impulses. Paul remembered that as a youth he had envied friends whose parents had set limits on their behavior. He then summarized his psychodynamics as follows: "I must have thought that my father got his leg injured in the war because he was too aggressive and that he became passive so he would not be further mutilated. I, thus, learned to inhibit myself so that I would not get injured like he was. When I feel I have too much sex-drive, I use guilt as a tool to stop me. Then I feel frustrated and angry. My guilt is my control mechanism. As a child, I must have thought that girls got their penises cut off because they had been too aggressive."

Paul then remembered that when his car skidded off the road, he had the thought, "I should *cut off* my high-powered sports car," when he had meant to think, "I should *sell off* my high-powered sports car." To this mental parapraxis, he associated that his sports car symbolized his male potency, and that, unconsciously, his thought: "cut off my high-powered sports car" had meant: "cut off my high-powered *penis*." He then realized that, beginning when he was a small boy, he had *cut off his competitive sexual desires* for his mother so that his penis would not be *cut off*. These associations explained to him why, after any success, he had felt depressed and inadequate and had become more inhibited.

Eight months later, Paul dreamed that *he was having intercourse with a woman who resembled his mother. He saw her naked. When he realized that he had made love with his mother, he sobbed. Then a large bodyguard, with a big knife said, "We 'cut off' things for that."* Associating to this dream, Paul remembered that when he was six he had dreamed that *a big giant was chasing him to 'smash' him.* Paul understood that his current dream expressed his childhood wish to be sexual with his mother and that both dreams expressed his fear and guilt-motivated wish that his father had more aggressively set limits on Paul's behavior and on his hidden sexual impulses.

Two years after having this dream, Paul became aware that he had been wishing that I would become an omnipotent, limit-setting father-figure for him. He recalled that, as a child, after he had given up trying to get external restrictions from his father, he had displaced his wish for such limits onto what he called "the Old Testament God of Retribution." He then realized that he wanted me to have this Godlike magical power so that the anger that he felt toward me, which he felt to be magically omnipotent, would not harm me. These thoughts led Paul to remember an important, formerly repressed, event from his fifth year:

While Paul's father was pitching a baseball to Paul to teach him how to bat a ball, Paul had the thought, "If I bat the ball, and it hits my father in the head, he will die. Then I will have my mother all to myself again." Paul became horrified of this thought, dropped the bat, and ran, crying, into their house. He refused to tell his puzzled father why he had run into the house. Subsequently Paul repressed this entire event.

Paul realized that he had repressed this event because he had been terrified that his hostile thought might have magical-wish-power and come true. He now understood why, after that event, he had always refused to participate in any competitive sport like baseball.

Soon after remembering this event, Paul awoke in a panic from a dream in which *someone was pulling something over his head, and there were many tubes over him*. Associating to this dream, he remembered that when he had his tonsils out at age three, a *mask and tubes* were put over his head. He now also remembered that, following the baseball bat incident, he had thought that his tonsillectomy had been a punishment, *in advance*, by the Old Testament God of Retribution for his *subsequent* wish to kill his father. Up to this point this thought had been repressed.

Paul then became aware that whenever he had wanted to outdo someone, he had inhibited, underestimated, and humbled himself because he feared that he would harm them with his unconscious "magical-balloon-power" and "magical-bat power." One way he had inhibited himself was by obsessing about what he called "the fearsome, punitive, Old Testament God of Retribution." This resulted in his having low self-esteem. Once Paul understood this, he stopped being submissive and became appropriately aggressive. He stopped letting others take credit for his work, quit his job, and developed his own business. His income then more than quadrupled. Also, because Paul no longer feared that his anger had magical consequences, he could better understand and deal with his anger. He could now play a father role and direct and instruct his sons and employees without feeling guilty. His colleagues, employees, and sons responded to this change by becoming more open and comfortable with him. They also became more productive.

Later, Paul became angry with me for canceling an appointment. He said that in my absence he had inappropriate sexual impulses, and he complained that I had not been there to help him counteract them. It became clear to him that he was re-experiencing, with me, the angry feelings he had toward his father for not stopping him from sharing a bedroom with his mother.

THE PSYCHOANALYSIS OF PAUL'S OBSESSION WITH ROBOTS, DUMMIES, MANIKINS, DOLLS, PUPPETS, AND MEN DRESSED AS WOMEN

Thus, as Paul recognized and worked through his angry feelings toward me in his father-transference, he became more aware of his anger toward his father for having been silent, passive, distant, and seemingly indifferent. Simultaneously, both his sexual interest in women and his obsessional thoughts about whether or not they were robots, dummies, manikins, dolls, puppets, or men dressed as women increased. Associating to this paradoxical increase, he reminisced about the second time, when he was five, that he saw a little girl's genital area. He said that he did not then know that females were born without penises, and so he had made the fearful assumption that their penises had been "cut off." Shortly after this, he saw his mother put a girl hand puppet on her hand and then remove it. It was then that he created the reassuring hypothesis that the little girl had not had her penis cut off, but that it was hidden behind a girl-puppet-costume, just as his mother's hand had been hidden behind the girl-hand-puppet.[5]

Thereafter, he used his girl-puppet-costume hypothesis to cover-over his terrifying assumption that females were castrated males. However, unconsciously, he continued to doubt the truth of his hypothesis, and this doubt manifested itself in his conscious symptom of doubting about whether women were puppets, dummies, manikins, dolls, robots, or men dressed as women. After Paul attained this new psychodynamic insight, he again remembered the fantasy that he had first had when he was five and that he frequently had during latency: *He would find a girl who had been injured by an automobile accident and put her back together.* He now clearly understood that this fantasy had been

---

[5]Rangell described a patient who suffered from a doll phobia. In his patient, too, the doll symbolically represented the penis and at the same time the female genital (Rangell 1952).

motivated by his unconscious wish to restore the penises that he believed females had lost.

Paul now understood that his fear of robots, dummies, manikins, dolls, puppets, men dressed in women's clothing, and disabled persons had been a conscious, symptomatic cover-up of his unconscious belief that females were castrated males. Gradually, Paul's conscious understanding that females were born without penises overcame his emotionally powerful, frightening, unconscious, childhood assumption that females were males that had been castrated.

Paul then asked himself why he became disgusted, angry, and turned-off sexually, when he saw a woman wearing sexually provocative clothing, but became sexually aroused when he put on similar clothing. Working on this paradoxical behavior we discovered that it began while he shared the bedroom with his mother. At that time he had not wanted to know that he had sexual feelings for her or that she lacked a penis. So he had defended himself from this knowledge by *isolating* his sexual feelings from her and *displacing* them onto her sexually provocative underclothing. After that, without allowing himself to consciously know either that he was sexually aroused by his mother or that she lacked a penis, he was able to put on her underclothing, look at himself in a mirror, unconsciously see an image of his mother with a penis hidden beneath her underclothing, and successfully masturbate to orgasm. Subsequently, he repeated this pattern of behavior with other women that he found attractive.

Paul now understood why he had always been so curious about, and sexually turned on by, women's sexy underwear, robots, dummies, manikins, dolls, puppets, and men dressed as women. He also understood why he had always felt that simulated women were ideal and perfect, whereas real women were imperfect: Real women were imperfect because they lacked penises, whereas simulated women were perfect because they had penises hidden beneath their costumes. Soon Paul became aware that when he looked at himself in a mirror while wearing sexually provocative underclothing, he was unconsciously visualizing his mother, who he closely resembled. He then also realized that, although *consciously he had felt shame* for wearing women's underclothing to masturbate, *unconsciously he had felt guilt* for fantasying that he was having sex with his mother.

Paul now allowed himself to realize that his mother had been sexually seductive with him. He remembered that before he was six, whenever his father was away, his mother had undressed in front of him and had slept with him. Even during his puberty his mother had twice come out of the shower naked in front of him. She always wore extremely short skirts and low-cut blouses.

I asked Paul if his mother was currently dressing provocatively and behaving seductively with him. He became angry and accused me of pushing him. I suggested that perhaps he was angry with me, as he had been with his father, for not preventing him from getting too close to his mother. Several months later, Paul finally overcame his resistance and was able to observe the following about his mother's current behavior and clothing:

(1) Paul learned from his sons, that his mother had been excessively seductive with them.

(2) His mother sat next to him on the couch and hugged him while they watched television. She was wearing a sheer blouse and very short shorts. He felt "embarrassed and uncomfortable" and "thought she was going too far." After his mother went home, Jane put her hand down Paul's shirt, and he became inappropriately anxious and angry. He realized that he had switched his discomfort over his sexual feelings toward his mother to Jane.

(3) Another time his mother sat next to him and "pulled her skirt up to her crotch." Paul was surprised that his father "did not seem to notice, or object to," his mother's "inappropriate, immodest behavior."

(4) He was surprised to note that his mother was "flagrantly seductive and dressed in an outrageously sexually-provocative way." It amazed him that he had never before allowed himself to be aware of this. He then became aware that part of the reason that men who dressed in women's clothing had fascinated and frightened him was because their exaggeratedly feminine attire and behavior had reminded him of his mother.

(5) Paul noticed that when his mother kissed him she put her tongue into his mouth while pressing both her breasts and her pelvis against him. He then realized that his mother had always hugged and kissed him this way, but he had "never allowed himself to notice this before." He added that he had never seen his parents hug or kiss.

(6) Paul then again went over the many episodes in which his mother had been overly seductive with him, and he became aware that, whenever he had shown any indication of having become sexually aroused by her, she had withdrawn from him. This had made him feel rejected, abandoned, and forsaken, and led him to assume that all

women would reject him if he became aroused. Paul had felt that if he sexually enjoyed his penis he would lose his mother. Thus like all the other patients presented in this book, Paul felt that he had to either give up his penis or give up his mother. He was caught between his castration anxiety and his separation anxiety.

After gaining all these insights, Paul no longer had to fantasy that he was wearing Jane's underclothing in order to sustain his erection during intercourse. Instead, he could now think of Jane, maintain his erection, and ejaculate. He was even able to remain aroused when he looked at her genitals.

THE TERMINATION PHASE OF PAUL'S PSYCHOANALYSIS

Paul told me that he felt he was ready to stop his psychoanalysis because his new insights had relieved him of the problems that brought him into psychoanalytic therapy. He also now knew that his mother, not he, had caused his adopted son's problems. He now fully understood that he had been compelled to masturbate in women's underclothing to prove to himself that women had penises hidden under their panties. He also knew that his mother dressed in extravagantly erotic clothing both to demonstrate her power over men and to deny her feeling that she was inferior because she lacked a penis. Now he could look at Jane's genitalia without feeling disgust, dizziness, or testicular discomfort. Robots, dummies, manikins, dolls, puppets, and men dressed as women no longer frightened, fascinated, or aroused him.

Six days before our final appointment, Paul's father died unexpectedly of a heart attack. Paul became sad, and he worried that he "might begin to suffer from oedipal guilt." Although he did experience some guilt, he was consciously aware that he was in no way responsible for his father's death. He realized that his guilt was due to his formerly unconscious, magical wish that his father would die. That night Paul had a wish-fulfilling dream that *his father was alive*. Paul understood that his unreasonable apprehension about now having to manage his mother's finances was a manifestation of his old guilt over his former wish to take his father's place with her. Paul said he would have been surprised if he had not felt some guilt.

Paul regretted that he had to lose and grieve over both his father and me simultaneously, and he worried that he might need to continue his analysis for several extra months. However, he decided to end on the date we planned. Two days before finishing, Paul **dreamed** that *his parents were together, and that he was off alone.*

During Paul's last session, he said, "My father's death overshadows my grief over losing you. If I do have trouble, especially with my mother, I may call you."

It has been more than fourteen-years since Paul finished his analysis, and he has not called. I called him to see how he was doing, and he said that none of his symptoms had returned.

PAUL'S DEFENSE MECHANISMS AND RESISTANCES

Repression, isolation, and doubting were Paul's predominant defense mechanisms. Between the age of three and thirteen, Paul had often seen that females lacked penises. Each time he had promptly **repressed** what he had seen. Early in his analysis, whenever he remembered one of these experiences, he would promptly repress and forget it. Once he learned about his unconscious fear of castration, he no longer had to repress these memories. Isolation was Paul's second line of defense. After he ceased to repress a memory, he often promptly isolated it. Thus, first he would alternately remember and then forget a memory. Then he would alternately connect and then isolate a memory. When he connected (unisolated) a memory, he would say he was "replacing a missing piece of a picture puzzle." After I repeatedly pointed out his use of these two defenses, his formerly repressed or isolated memories became consistently both conscious and connected. Thus, Paul's repressed, unconscious memories of past and present experiences and fantasies emerged as disconnected, anachronistic, meaningless fragments. He and I gradually assembled these newly conscious fragments into a meaningfully organized, chronologically coherent, genetic-dynamic explication of both his distressing symptoms and his maladaptive behaviors. This newly conscious knowledge was curative for Paul.

When he obsessed about whether either a real woman or a simulated woman was real or fake, he was using the defense mechanism of doubting. When Paul experienced disgust, he was using reaction formation.

Paul's unconscious magical thinking, i.e., his belief that he possessed "balloon-on-a-stick power" and "baseball-bat power," was a major determinant of his neurotic symptoms. Near the end of his analysis, Paul said that he was sad that he had to give up his unconscious belief that he had magical, omnipotent-wish-power, because that meant that he would also have to give up fulfilling his unconscious, childhood oedipal wish to supplant his father and marry his mother.

Genetic-Dynamic Formulation

Before the age of four, Paul had been indoctrinated with the idea that his wishes would magically come true if he prayed to God.

Early in his fifth year, while Paul was watching his mother *remove* a little girl's diaper, he saw that the little girl lacked a penis. He thought that her penis had been *removed,* and had the terrifying thought that his penis could also be *removed*. Several days later, he watched his mother *remove* a hand puppet. This reminded him both of the diaper being *removed* and his thought that the little girl's penis had been *removed*, and he again became terrified. Paul then repressed his frightful thought that his penis could be *removed*, concealing it behind the following defensive rationalization: He hypothesized that just as his mother's hand and fingers had been concealed behind the hand puppet, the little girl's penis must have been concealed behind a "skintight girl-puppet-costume." After that, whenever he saw a puppet, robot, dummy, manikin, or doll that resembled a human, he would obsess, back and forth, whether it was a *real* human or a *simulated* one. In puberty, Paul also began to obsess whether attractive women were *real* or *simulated* humans.

Late in his fifth year, Paul was in a grocery store, playing with his penis with one hand and a balloon-on-a-stick with his other hand. While fantasying that his balloon-on-a-stick was a magical wand, he pointed it toward a stack of Coca-Cola bottles and wished that they would fall down without their having to be touched either by him or by his magical wand. To his amazement, even though it was not touched, the stack immediately collapsed. This experience led him to believe that his wishes had magical power. Soon after this experience, while he was batting baseballs toward his father, Paul had the thought that if the ball hit his father on the head and killed him, Paul would again have his mother all to himself again. He feared that this thought, like the wish that he had toward the Coca-Cola bottles, might also come true. Terrified, he dropped his bat, and ran into the house crying. Paul then prayed to the "all-powerful, Old Testament, punitive God of Retribution," asking him to counteract his malicious magical wish. Paul then unconsciously came to believe that his tonsillectomy at age three had been an anticipatory magical punishment for his subsequent wish to kill his father. Toward the end of his analysis Paul described these events as follows: "Both the balloon-on-the-stick and the baseball-bat events occurred at about the same time that I observed that the little girl lacked a penis. I linked these three events with my tonsillectomy, my seeing my mother menstruate, and my father's mutilated leg—and that set the stage for all that happened within me afterwards."

At age thirteen, when Paul's genital sexual drive began to heighten, he and his mother moved 200 miles away from his father. There, he shared a bedroom with his mother and twice saw her naked. Once he saw her naked pubic area and became disgusted. Then, one day, her skirt rode up as she was getting out of her car, and he saw her stockings, garter belt, and sheer under panties. Because he did not want to admit to himself that he had been sexually aroused by seeing this, he unconsciously *isolated* his sexual feelings from her genitals and *displaced* them onto her underclothing. His mother, thus, was seductive—not castrating. That evening he put on her stockings, garter belt, and sheer under panties, and while looking at himself in a mirror, he masturbated to orgasm. Since he closely resembled his mother, when he looked at himself in the mirror with her under panties, garter belt, and stockings on, unconsciously he saw his mother with a penis hidden under her skintight-girl-underclothing. This was both the first time he cross-dressed and the first time he masturbated to orgasm.

After ejaculating, he unconsciously feared that his childhood wish to replace his father with his mother might be magically coming true. To protect himself from becoming consciously aware of both this unconscious wish and his unconscious fear of retaliatory castration, he employed the same defensive rationalization that he had created to cover up and repress the fear of castration that he had experienced at age five when he saw that the two little girls lacked penises. When five, he had unconsciously rationalized that the *two little girls had penises hidden under their skintight-girl-puppet-costumes*. Now he unconsciously rationalized that his *mother had a penis hidden under her underclothing*. After that, in order to have an orgasm, he always had to either wear a woman's sexy underclothing while looking at himself in a mirror or fantasy that he was doing so.

Thus, Paul's transvestite cross-dressing: (1) Kept his castration anxiety unconscious by denying that the little girls, his mother, and other women lacked penises, (2) Kept his separation anxiety unconscious by repressing his fear that his mother would reject him for desiring her sexually, (3) Unconsciously discharged his impulse to have sex with his mother, and (4) Punished him for unconsciously wishing to have sex with his mother.

REFERENCE

RANGELL, L. (1952). The Analysis of a Doll Phobia *International Journal of Psychoanalysis* 33:43–53.

TREATMENT OF BOYS WITH THE GENDER-IDENTITY DISORDER OF TRANSSEXUALISM[1]

K nowing how similar symptoms develop in childhood is important in formulating the etiology of adult male transsexualism. I have observed transsexual symptoms in two male children whom I treated with psychoanalysis. I did not have to speculate retrospectively because the symptoms manifested in the transference.

REVIEW OF THE LITERATURE

From 1905 to 1927 Freud gathered material that showed the traumatic effect on male children of their first view of female genitalia. In 1908, he said that, from knowing their own bodies, boys characteristically initially assume that everyone has a penis that is dominated by excitations and pleasure. In 1910, Freud further observed that the boy's fantasy that girls have penises may not be destroyed even after he observes their genitals. He may disavow, Freud said, ". . . his own sense-perceptions which showed him that the female genitals lack a penis and hold . . . fast to the contrary conviction" (Freud, 1940, p. 202). The boy may then create an unconscious fantasy in which he gives the woman a penis (Freud, 1927). For example, he may fantasy that a woman's penis is small, but that it will grow (Freud, 1908, p. 216), or he may fantasy that a woman has her bottom in front (Freud, 1918, p. 25) and a penis in back (Freud, 1918, p. 84). If a boy cannot convince himself with such fantasies, he may imagine that girls' genitals are wounds that remain where their penises were cut off. In 1905 Freud said, "The substitutes for this penis, which they [boys] find is missing in women, play a great part in determining the form taken by many perversions (p. 195)." Freud summarized, "Probably no male human-being is spared the fright of castration at the sight of a female genital. Why some people become homosexual as a consequence

---

[1]Previously published as Chapter 6 in the book *Sexual Deviation,* Third Edition, edited by Ismond Rosen, Oxford University Press. 1966.

of that impression, while others fend it off by creating a fetish, and the great majority surmount it, we are frankly not able to explain . . . among all the factors at work, we do not yet know those which are decisive for the rare pathological results" (1927, p. 154). Thus, according to Freud (1927), young boys can develop a tendency toward perversion if they are traumatized by the sight of female genitalia.

The work of Sperling and Greenson in this area exemplifies both Anna Freud's (1965/1966) and Geleerd's (1969) contention that knowledge derived from the psychoanalysis of children leads to better understanding of adult psychopathology. Almost all the psychoanalytic studies dealing with cross-dressing were on adults until Sperling (1963, 1968) and Greenson (1966) reported analyses of cross-dressing children. Their studies provide data on the early pathological picture and intrapsychic structure of feminine boys. While Greenson (1966) stressed the therapeutic benefit of identification with a strong masculine figure, he recognized the transference manifestations of the pathological relationship with the mother. He felt that confrontation and interpretation in his analysis of the boy improved the pathological relationship with the mother.

Stoller (1967) said that transsexuals are cross-dressers who wish to live and be accepted as members of the opposite sex. They complain they are females trapped in an anatomically normal male body. Stoller referred to a person's self-designation, irrespective of their anatomy, as their "core gender identity." This core gender identity is produced by environmental and intrapsychic effects. He (1973) described three mechanisms that produce normal gender identity: (1) the anatomy and physiology of external genital organs, (2) the attitudinal influences of parents, siblings, and peers, and (3) a "biological force" which, although hidden from conscious and unconscious awareness, nonetheless seems to provide some drive energy for gender identity.

Newman and Stoller (1971) found several highly specific factors in the early developmental histories of adult male transsexuals. Stoller (1975b) and Green, Stoller, and Newman (1972, 1976) found these same common features in the early developmental histories of young boys with transsexual symptoms. Stoller (1973, 1975b) described these features as follows: By age one, the boys showed signs of feminine gender behavior. By age two or three they were unusually good-looking, preferred dressing and playing as girls, expressed the wish to have a female body, and were not thought to be psychotic. Stoller (1973, 1975b) described their mothers as follows: They had strong bisexual characteristics, took almost all their babies to bed with them, exhibited considerable penis envy, and used their sons as phallic substitutes. They also encouraged an unending "blissful symbiosis" by not allowing their sons to experience frustration.[2] The fathers of transsexuals, if not physically absent, were absent psychologically. According to Stoller, the fathers served neither as models for masculine identification nor as protectors from the mother's feminizing efforts at symbiotic merger.

In Mahler's (Mahler, Pine, and Bergman, 1975) clinical experience, transsexualism is related to the mother's unconscious attitude toward her own self, especially her belief in her femininity or lack of it, her feminine self-esteem; her castration conflicts (p. 214); her penis awe (Greenacre, 1953); her penis envy; and her defenses related to all these. In summary, the discoveries made by Mahler, Pine, and Bergman (1975) regarding gender identity in boys include: (1) Gender identity in the boy asserts itself with less conflict if the mother respects and enjoys the boy's phallicity, especially in the second half of the third year. (2) Identification with the father or with an older brother facilitates a boy's male gender identity. (3) Gender identity is impeded when the mother interferes with the boy's autonomy. This is particularly true if the mother is unable to relinquish to him, his body, and the ownership of his penis.

Jacobson (1964), Roiphe and Galenson (1973), and Abelin (1977) state that the failure of the father to aid the child in achieving separation and autonomy from the mother is evident in sexual perversions. Pruett and Dahl (1982) reported on the psychotherapy of three boys less than six years old who cross-dressed and exhibited feminine behavior. The boys' previous behavioral shaping had not helped them resolve their conflicts. Pruett and Dahl used interpretation, clarification, and the relationship with the therapist to enable the boys' egos "to cope in more appropriate ways."

Green (1987) studied two behaviorally different groups of feminine boys with questionnaires, psychological tests, and interviews. He based his conclusions not on the unconscious determinants of these boys' feminine symptomatology, but on their conscious thoughts and overt behavior. He used behavior modification to treat these boys and their parents, and helped them adjust to society. Green said that this treatment approach showed no major impact on these boys' sexual orientation. The therapy

---

[2]In my two cases I did not observe any blissful symbiosis, but neither mother could say "No" to her son.

did not interrupt their progression from "feminine" boys to homosexual or bisexual men (1987, p. 318).

Socarides (1970) considered transsexualism to be like all other perversions: It is the outcome of intrapsychic conflict and affords both sexual release and ego survival. For Socarides, transsexualism represents a regression to an earlier phase, in which there is both desire for, and dread of, a merger with the mother. This regression is fostered by a mother who has great difficulty separating from her child. She holds on to her child, preventing him from taking the developmental step of differentiating from her. This exerts a pathological, feminizing influence on her son's gender identity. This pathological sense of feminine gender, of being feminine and linked to mother, conflicts with the child's emerging awareness of the genital aspects of his body image and with his phase-appropriate tendencies to disidentify. This engenders a severe internalized conflict between a desire for merger with the mother and a fear of loss of sense of self. The latter blends with castration anxiety on a pre-oedipal level (Roiphe and Galenson, 1973).

Socarides (1970), Limentani (1979), Loeb and Shane (1982), and Loeb (1992) observed that transsexuals grow up in maternal environments that conflict with their biological maleness. These observations contradict Stoller's view (1973, 1975a, 1975b) that transsexuals never had any masculinity, castration anxiety, or intrapsychic conflict.

Person and Ovesey (1974a, 1974b) considered the transsexual wish to be the nucleus of a syndrome. They viewed transsexualism as a symptomatic compromise formation in which the threat is from early maternal abandonment, and the defensive fantasy is of a symbiotic merger with the mother. Thus, in the transsexual, sexuality is largely sacrificed for the security of getting needs met. Volkan and Berent (1976) found conflict around the wish for sex reassignment surgery was not expressed directly, but appeared in dreams and in the behavior of the adult transsexuals. P. Tyson (1982) proposed that the developmental line of gender identity be seen as (1) core gender identity, (2) gender role identity, and (3) sexual partner orientation. The interaction of these factors produces, she said, the final "broad sense of gender identity."

Harrison and Cain (1968), Meyer (1974), and Walinder and Thuwe (1975) found histories of abandonment, disregard, and abusive language, such as calling the child "scum," rather than extraordinary symbiosis in the history (p. 387). Jon Meyer (1982) comprehensively reviewed the existing theories of transsexualism. He examined and followed 526 patients who wished to have their genitalia and other physical attributes modified to that of the opposite sex. He found an absence in their history of extraordinary symbiosis. Meyer did not find patients that fit Stoller's criteria for "true" transsexualism (p. 386). Although Meyer (1982) regretted that he did not have the opportunity to psychoanalyze the patients that he evaluated, my analyses of two boys support his conclusions, as well as those of Loeb and Shane (1992).

Jon Meyer and Duplin (1985) observed twelve children who engaged in cross-gender behavior. As much as possible, they maintained neutrality and avoided the education, explanation and suggestion that Green (1974) used. They tentatively concluded that gender-disturbed behavior is due to early traumatic experiences that result in intrapsychic conflicts. The traumatic experience is reinforced by repeated assaults by the parental object, who may be a mother, sister, grandmother, or teacher. They said: "Failure of object constancy in these children was apparent in their object hunger, narcissistic vulnerability, and separation anxiety, and in a neediness reflected in wanting to 'get things'." In none of the male children was there evidence of a "blissful symbiosis" of the type called for in Stoller's formulations (p. 260).

The wish of a six-year-old boy, treated by Sylvia Brody, to be transsexual, was observed by his teachers, not his parents. "In his early childhood, the mother said, he had clung to her exceedingly, which she had greatly deplored. In contrast she was pleased and proud of his obedience. She had always insisted on his being orderly and controlled, for she could not bear boys who were 'rough or wild.' She wished him to be strong, however, and so believed it best not to show him tenderness or sentiment. He had come to perceive normal phallic striving as a threat to his allegiance to her, and had sadly resigned himself to exclusion from her emotional life. The father was utterly remote from him affectively and took no interest in the child's daily experiences, but rather was devoted to pleasures with mother alone. The boy had come to feel abandoned by both parents, and to nourish the fantasy that had he been born a girl, he would have been insured against their chronic neglect of his feelings" (1994).

Coates, et al. (1991) reported on a three-year-old boy, Colin, with gender identity disorder who believed that if you wore girls' clothes you could really become a girl. He did this to please his mother, repair her depression, and cause his withdrawn mother to return. On the Rorschach they found themes of dread, separation, and loss. Representations of females were idealized and valued, while representations of males were absent. Clinically, Colin's cross-gender behavior increased when his mother was inaccessible due to separation or depression. The inaccessibility of both parents left Colin feeling abandoned. Coates, et al. (1991) said that the cross-gender fantasy allows the child to manage traumatic levels of anxiety.

CLINICAL CASE: CARLOS[3]

Method

My first case was a five-year-old boy, Carlos, who wished to be a girl (Loeb & Shane 1982). I saw the child when I was a child-analytic candidate and Shane supervised me. The child fit the criteria that Stoller (1973, 1975b) had identified for diagnosing a primary transsexual condition.

Shane and I worked psychoanalytically with this highly motivated boy using as few parameters as possible. We worked on giving him insight into the intrapsychic conflicts that had produced his psychopathology. This eventually reduced his anxiety and diminished his symptoms. Although we had to interrupt the treatment after only eight months, the patient had significantly worked through the conflict that led to his transsexual wish. Shane and I are convinced that this boy would have become an adult transsexual without our psychoanalytic intervention. This case demonstrated that conflicts can exist in a transsexual child and that psychoanalytic treatment can resolve these conflicts and lead to the cessation of symptoms (Loeb and Shane, 1982).

When I began this treatment, I knew little about transsexual children. Shane recommended that, instead of reading the literature, I just treat the child following a scientific psychoanalytic investigative technique. After I completed the analysis, I read the literature and was surprised to learn that Stoller (1975b p. 94) had said that the pathology was pre-conflictual in these children.

Carlos's History

Carlos, a good-looking boy of five years, ten months, was brought for consultation by his forty-five-year-old parents both because he wished to be his father's daughter, and because he felt women were

---

[3]A version of this case was presented at the Annual Meeting of the American Psychoanalytic Association, Atlanta, Georgia, May 1978 and then published (Loeb & Shane, 1982).

better than men. His mother became worried when he became anxious and did not want to go to school after his kindergarten classmates teased him by calling him "Conchita." Although she had at first encouraged his feminine behavior, she no longer took lightly his wearing women's clothing, makeup, and jewelry, and his playing exclusively with girls. His father became upset and angry when Carlos said he wanted to be a girl and not have a penis.

Mrs. N., who came from Argentina, had separated from Mr. N., an American, and had returned to Argentina to live with her sister and mother to give birth to Carlos. She remained with them until Carlos was two-and-a-half years old. Carlos walked at ten-and-a-half months, talked by one-year, and was weaned at two-and-a-half years. He was toilet trained, without difficulty, at age three. Between the ages of one and two, Carlos pleased his mother by putting on her lingerie and lipstick, playing with her lace, and imitating her voice.

When Carlos and his mother reunited with Mr. N. in the United States, a male figure entered Carlos's life for the first time. Up to that time he had slept in his mother's bed because she "could not say 'no'." When he was moved out of his mother's bed into his own room, he screamed for hours saying that he was afraid of the dark, bodily injury, and monsters. Carlos's father tried to stop his mother both from taking Carlos to bed and from supporting his effeminate behavior, but his mother would not change. Father then withdrew from the family and often left home. His parents continued to separate and reunite, and when father was gone, Carlos became anxious and sad, and his effeminate behavior increased. He would put his mother's clothing on while telling her how lucky she was *not* to have a "wiener." His father became alarmed when, at age three, Carlos was still dressing as a girl, pretending he had big breasts, and playing only with girls. At age four, after his brother was born, while hiding his penis between his legs, Carlos would "spy" on his mother while she undressed or bathed. He would say that he was ashamed of his penis and that he would like to cut it off. His parents were frightened by these thoughts and by his occasionally cutting things with scissors, such as window screens. I thought that this might mean that when he saw that his mother did not have a penis he experienced castration anxiety and turned his mother's aggression toward himself. His younger brother had shown no signs of transsexualism by age five.

Mrs. N., an attractive, though sloppily dressed, woman was anxious in our first interview. The eldest of two daughters, she and Carlos were both named after her father. Following her father's death in an accident when she was a teenager, Mrs. N. assumed her father's dominant position in the family.

Mr. N. was a tall, handsome lawyer with a suave manner. His relationship to his own mother was highly ambivalent. Mr. N's stepfather died while his wife was pregnant with Carlos, and Mr. N. left his wife to care for his mother.

Diagnosis and Treatment Plan

After several interviews with the family, Shane and I concluded that, despite Carlos's blatant transsexual symptoms, he clearly manifested intrapsychic conflicts. We, therefore, decided that I would try to help him with a psychoanalysis. His parents, both of whom were eager to see their child find relief from his suffering, were placed in psychotherapy with a psychoanalytically oriented social worker. While this paper will focus on Carlos's treatment, it is important to note that in her own psychotherapy Mrs. N. developed some intellectual understanding of (1) her degrading attitude toward her husband, (2) her feminizing, overprotective, infantilizing closeness to Carlos, and (3) her resentment toward her own father. However, she still maintained a religious conviction that her son was "possessed" by a woman. Mr. N.'s attendance in psychotherapy was infrequent. Nevertheless, he noticed that his son did much better when he spent more time with the family. Mr. N. consequently vowed not to leave them for extended periods, and more or less kept to this promise.

Eventually, each of the basic criteria cited by Stoller for diagnosing a transsexual became a major focus in the transference, just as each of these criteria had been a focal point for the development of a conflict in Carlos. Stoller's criteria include: (1) an unending desire to be with and be attached to his mother, (2) an absent father, (3) a mother who has a castrating attitude toward men, and (4) an exceptional beauty. The conflicts we saw in Carlos included: (1) his difficulty staying close to his castrating mother, (2) his father's absence, which made him conflicted about assuming his father's masculine identity, (3) his conflicted wish to be castrated, which was promoted by his mother's continuously castrating attitude toward his father and him, and (4) his "special beauty," which facilitated both his identification with his attractive mother and her identification with him.

Course of the Analysis

At the onset of the analysis, Carlos would not leave his mother to go with me into my office. He finally did so when I offered to share my soda with him. Throughout his short analysis, he periodically asked for a soda from me. This came to represent oral closeness to me. Occasionally, even well into treatment, he would run out of my office to look for his mother.

While making feminine gestures and imitating my voice, he began his play therapy by drawing female clothespin figures with breasts, long hair, high heels, and black pelvic areas. He also drew his father with the same fetish-like high heels.

Through play activities Carlos worked within the developing transference relationship on his unresolved fear of being abandoned. He would play hide-and-seek; or he would tie a baby doll to a mother doll and block the windows and doors of the doll house to prevent any separation; or he would play at being the Flying Nun, who represented both his wish to identify with his phallic mother and fly toward or away from her. He also took my girl doll home with him so he could work on what he called his "worries." In the transference he was using my doll as a transitional object to keep me with him.

Early in the analysis Carlos would alternate between (1) getting physically close to me and acting feminine, passive, and dependent, and (2) pushing me away from him and acting more masculine, aggressive, and independent. When acting more masculine, he would make messes and order me to clean them up. At first, I just observed this alternating sequence of behavior and did not respond to it. Eventually, I began to interpret to him that he seemed to have a conflict between wanting to be close to me by acting like a submissive, dependent girl and wanting to push me away by acting aggressive, dominant, and controlling. Later, after he acknowledged this, I also began to tell him that I did not have to do everything he told me to do when he acted like an aggressive, dominant and controlling boy. He would respond that I "had better behave" and follow his wishes. On one such occasion, he said he would call a policeman to force me to do what he wanted me to do. I interpreted to him that this showed that he wished to have his father, who was a type of law-enforcing agent, there with him. He responded by laughingly and deliberately spilling soda on his clothing. I asked him if he was keeping his father with him by acting like his father, and I reminded him that he had told me that his mother had recently become angry with his father and had criticized him for spilling soda on his tie. I also asked him if he might be testing me to see if I, a female like his mother, would put him down for spilling soda. When I first made interpretations like this, Carlos felt I was criticizing him for wanting to be like his father. He responded by first becoming passive, acquiescent, and effeminate, and then later becoming angry and striking out at me. As we repeatedly worked on this behavior in the transference, he gradually became more masculine and aggressive toward me, but he continued to fear that I would reject him for doing so. Eventually, he realized that he feared that I would reject him if he were aggressive or masculine with me because his mother had repeatedly rejected both him and his father if they acted aggressive or manly. As we worked on this, Carlos gradually became more masculine with me and less acquiescent or hostile toward me. Simultaneously, he was beginning to play more with boys than with girls at school.

Thus, as Carlos began to see me less as his castrating mother and more as my real self, he became less hostile, passive-dependant and effeminate and more autonomous with me. He also began to notice my actual reactions and expressed surprise when he learned that I had needs and wishes and pains distinct from his own. For example, he realized that he could be thirsty and I did not need to drink. During the middle phase of the analytic work, he would climb precariously on my furniture as if to test his capacity to be independent. Whenever I was forced to protect him by breaking his falls, he would regress. He would speak in a feminine voice, gesture like a woman, me, and call himself "gorgeous." This behavior led us to realize that he did not enjoy the role of a child dependent on an adult. Instead, under these circumstances he felt threatened by me, whom he saw as his mother who was demanding that he merge with her and give up his nascent autonomy and masculinity. Once, as he was falling, I protectively caught him. As he was gathering his balance, he acted effeminate and said he was gorgeous. I disagreed (said "No" to him) and said that I thought he was handsome and that usually girls are called gorgeous. The next day he gallantly brought me candy and a Valentine's Day card. He realized that it was all right with me for him to be close to me and still be a boy. After much discussion about being a handsome boy and not a gorgeous girl, he then began to aggressively renounce his feminine gender identity. Following this insight, he stopped sharing what happened in his analysis with his mother.

Soon Carlos became phallically competitive with me in the analytic situation, and he asked to take home my pens and my string. He gave

them to his father, hoping to transmit my phallic strength—as manifested in my ability to say "No" to him—to his father. Carlos and his
father used my string to fly kites. In addition, Carlos was now taking my
dolls home to bed with him and using them to masturbate. These transitional objects continued to be substitutes for me. Thus, he was relinquishing his defenses against his biologically-determined genital desires.
These desires had previously conflicted with his internalized representation of his mother, and this had led him to develop his transsexual
symptoms. Later, there was a second significant developmental shift
for Carlos away from an identification with his mother and toward a phallic identification with his father. This was shown when Carlos began
sleeping with his father's Navy torpedo pin instead of with my dolls.
Carlos showed further indications that he was moving toward the phallic-oedipal stage: He told his parents that he no longer wanted to be a
girl, but would rather be a boy-angel and fly. More directly, he told me
he wanted to be a boy and be a pilot. Symbolically, flying combined
Carlos's phallic desires with his wish to end his extreme closeness with
his mother. As Carlos became more phallic, he spoke about monsters
that came at night and disturbed his sleep. In his play with me, these
monsters represented his projected hostile-competitive, phallic-oedipal
wishes toward his father. After I interpreted his projected hostility in this
phallic-aggressive play, Carlos's oedipal anxiety gradually subsided,
and he again became able to sleep without fear.

Thus, we discovered that Carlos had an unconscious neurotic conflict between his biological genital feelings toward his mother and her
dislike of maleness, which he had internalized. This unconscious conflict
had manifested as his transsexual symptom.

Near the end of the analytic work, Carlos sat in my chair, put his feet
on my desk, and said: "You can't tell a book by its cover." He explained
that there was a child at school who dressed like a boy, played like a boy,
and had a boy's name. However, she was not a boy. She did not have a
penis, and that made the difference. Carlos's interpretation of this proverb
showed that he was now consciously aware of, and even able to abstractly
generalize about, his previously unconscious gender identity conflict
and confusion. Immediately after explaining this proverb, Carlos
exchanged the dolls he had taken from me for my cars. Later that week,
in an attempt to renounce his interest in being effeminate, he asked
his mother to put wings—like the ones the Flying Nun (a phallic woman)
had on her nun's cap on his baseball cap. Thus, he was relinquishing his

feminine identification with me as his mother, while retaining his identification with my phallic power through my cars and by putting wings on his baseball cap.

We had to prematurely interrupt Carlos's analysis when his father obtained a job in another city. I transferred Carlos to a male analyst in that city. During the last month of the analysis, Carlos stopped competing with me and frequently climbed on my lap. He often asked me to read to him the story of the "Magic Bus" that could go anywhere you wanted it to go, and the story of the elephant whose trunk did wonderful things. Carlos's free associations to these stories showed that they represented both his desire to be able to return to see me and his phallic ambitions. In his last session, Carlos expressed sadness about our forthcoming separation by doubting that there were guardian angels. I told him that he wished that I could magically go with him as a guardian angel, but that he really knew that he would have to take his "worries" to his new doctor. Carlos spent the rest of his final session drawing a picture of a female figure in a long dress. Unlike the earlier unisex pictures of men and women he had drawn with me, she had prominent hips and breasts and *no* high-heeled[4] shoes. He labeled the picture with my name. The picture showed that he had an awareness of me as a woman, separate and different from himself.

Follow-up of Carlos at Age Thirteen

Carlos's mother wrote that after the move, Mr. N. was hospitalized for hepatitis. Although Carlos continued to function well at home and at school, during the hospitalization he again began to play with the family of dolls I had given him. This enabled him to continue to work on his "worries" until he met with his new psychoanalyst. Presumably Carlos had responded to his father's absence with both separation and castration anxiety, but instead of defending against these anxieties and forming symptoms, he worked on them by playing with dolls—as he had done during the analysis. Carlos began his new analysis one month later.

During the subsequent four years with the new, male analyst, the analytic work continued with minimal parameters. Carlos remained highly motivated to seek relief from his anxiety-producing conflicts and rode 20 miles each way alone on public transportation to see his new analyst.

---

[4]In the case to follow, high-heeled shoes represented phallic substitutes in women.

Carlos's behavior continued slowly to become more masculine. Upon completion of his second analysis at age thirteen, his second analyst could not be certain that he would turn out to be completely heterosexual. However, Carlos was now definitely not transsexual. He still had some uncertainty about his femininity, but in a phase-appropriate way. His analyst felt that the stability of Carlos's masculine gender identity could best be assessed later in adolescence.

CLINICAL CASE: JAMES[5]

Method

James, the second young patient with transsexual symptoms that I analyzed, demonstrated our previously reported observation (Loeb and Shane, 1982) that transsexual symptoms can develop out of intrapsychic conflicts and can be resolved through a psychoanalysis. This case also provided further data as to the genesis of the transsexual symptom complex. In this psychoanalysis, I was abstinent and not benevolent or supportive. Both positive and negative transference feelings developed into a full-blown transference neurosis. As we analyzed the transference neurosis, we learned that he was acting out his identification with his aggressive, seductive, and castrating grandmother. When he came to understand his unconscious conflicts, we worked them through, and his transsexual symptoms vanished. At age ten, James finished his analysis. I saw him at age fifteen for a follow-up.

I tape-recorded the treatment. The recorder did not inhibit spontaneity in either James or me. Having the analysis on tape allowed James and me to go back and trace the development of themes that did not seem relevant when they first occurred. Although the accuracy of my written notes could be questioned, the accuracy of a tape recording could not. The recorded data show that James's unconscious intrapsychic conflicts led to his transsexual symptoms.

James's History

James, was an attractive four-year, eight-month-old boy, who, since the age of two-and-a-half, had wished to grow up and be a "mommy." He liked to pretend he had breasts, and to put on women's clothing and makeup. He preferred to play with girls. When he played with boys, he

---

[5]A version of this case was published (Loeb, 1992).

pretended he was a girl. He was now tired of pretending to be Wonder Woman and had intense concern about things that came apart. Recently, he had nightmares of policemen who fell on spiders and of a red crayfish monster that climbed on his mother's face and chased him.

James was adopted at birth when his adoptive parents' natural children were six, eight, and ten years old. His father, a financial executive, rarely spent time with James. Like James, his father had received little discipline from his parents. James's paternal grandfather had a congenitally shrunken arm. His work required him to take frequent trips, so he spent little time with his son or his grandchildren. James's paternal grandmother had low self-esteem and was very critical and condescending toward others. James's father had always avoided women who dressed attractively and seductively like his mother.

Between the ages of one-and-one-half and three-and-one-half, James, unlike his siblings, spent much time with his father's attractive mother. She lived nearby, and James's mother was happy to have a willing baby-sitter. His grandmother always dressed in "fancy," seductive, high-fashion clothing, and disrobed in front of James. He said that his "fancy grandmother" was a "nice lady" with a "yucky body." He said that ladies dressed "fancily" to cover their "yucky bodies." His paternal grandmother seldom said "No" to any of James's requests. She gave him whatever he wanted, including "Cool Whip" for lunch. She put makeup, jewelry, and girl's clothing on him and encouraged him to wear her high-heeled shoes.

As a toddler, James began to cover his chest with a towel after taking a bath. When three, he became preoccupied with Barbie dolls—especially their hair and high-heeled shoes. At three-and-one-half he began to put on women's clothing. His mother worried about his wanting to be a "fancy lady"; whereas James complained that his mother dressed too plainly. She was devoted to her home and family. Although a college graduate, she had low self-esteem. She regularly took James to bed with her when she found him crying after a nightmare. While sleepwalking, James went into the bathroom, flushed the toilet several times, and then went back to bed. At age four James was demanding; for James's parents, like his grandmother, rarely said "No" to him. His mother's parents spent little time with him.

When James's behavior became increasingly more feminine, and he began to put on his mother's lipstick, his father became upset, and his parents sought help. Because James's intrapsychic conflicts had interfered with his development, I started him in a psychoanalysis. At this time his parents also began psychoanalytic treatment to help their troubled marriage. During James's analysis, I met with both him and his parents whenever necessary.

Course of the Analysis

Intermittently, from the beginning of the analysis, James walked as though he were wearing high heels, alluringly fluttered his eyelashes, and repeated my words in an exaggeratedly feminine voice. After James complained that I, unlike his mother, did not try to read his thoughts and do what he wished, he turned away from me and played with two Barbie dolls. He dressed one in plain clothing and called her "mother." He called the other doll "queen-grandmother" and dressed her in a "fancy," low cut, strapless gown and high heels. Several times he showed how queen-grandmother's gown could slip down and expose her breasts, and he suggested that the gown should have straps. He ignored the Ken dolls. Often he asked me to take off my clothes. This was the beginning of his grandmother transference neurosis.

Several months into the analysis, James began breaking my toys, hitting me, spitting at me, putting his "snot" on me, and attempting to lift my skirt. He also tried to hit my eyes so I could not see what he was doing. When I asked him if he were angry at something, he would hit me again. I asked him why he could not tell me what he was angry about, and told him it was all right for him to hit the doll and we could talk about it but he could not hit me. He then temporarily stopped this abusive behavior. I asked him why he wanted to hurt me, and he replied that it was not he, but the monster that came in his nightmares who did these things. In one such nightmare, a half lady, half pinching-lobster-monster chased him. He woke up from the dream when the lobsters were running out of his mother's nose. He excitedly said, "Lobsters can pinch," and he continued to try to hurt me. Eventually, I told him that we could not work on his worries if he could not stop himself from trying to hurt me. I said that, if he continued, I would have to stop our session. When he did not stop, I told him that he was unable to say "No" to himself, and I opened the door and asked him to leave. Then, using feminine speech and mannerisms, he pleaded to be allowed to stay. His pleading did not work with me, and I insisted that he wait outside in the waiting room for his mother to pick him up. Thus, unlike his mother, who cried and ran away from his angry words and behavior, I confronted him and did not let him manipulate me and win. I tolerated and worked on his negative, hostile impulses in the transference, but I did not let him actually act out his angry thoughts and wishes toward me. I firmly adhered to this boundary, and this strengthened his therapeutic alliance, which was slowly evolving.

Castration themes then began to predominate in James's play. He pretended to be Dorothy in the Wizard of Oz, who was seeking *shoes* for herself, a *heart* for the Tin Man, a *brain* for the Straw Man, and *courage* for the Cowardly Lion, all representing power and penises. James also played that he was Cinderella, who repeatedly lost and recovered her shoe. One day I had a bandage on my foot and James became both gleeful and anxious.

Although, like his father, James had always feared dogs, in the second year of the analysis, he asked to have my large Great Dane come to a session. When I hesitatingly brought in the dog, I found James hiding in a corner. But James insisted that the dog continue to come to his sessions. Gradually, James became less frightened of the dog. After several months with the dog present, I noted that James was copying the dog's behavior. For example, when the Dane lay with his forelegs crossed in front of him and licked his paw, James would lay on his stomach with his arms crossed and lick his wrist. James was diminishing his anxiety by identifying with, and acting like, this feared object. I told James that he seemed no longer to be afraid of the dog because he was lying next to the dog and acting just like him. Observing how he got over his fear of the dog by imitating its behavior, helped James understand how he had gotten over his fear of his penis-less, castrating grandmother by imitating her behavior. In both instances, James was using the defense of *identification with the aggressor.*

James repeatedly disrupted his play by using the defense mechanisms of *denial, repression, doubting, doing and undoing, reaction-formation*, and *identification with the lost object*. He frequently *forgot* things he had learned. At times we would bring them back by playing the tape recordings. Like Carlos, he would *doubt*. He would express his central conflict by saying: "Yes, you have one; no, you don't have one. No, you don't love me because I have one; yes, you love me because I don't have one." He would *do and undo* by changing the doll's sex from boy to girl, or her clothing from fancy to plain, or her power from strong to weak. He would call me "Doctor Poop." Then, employing *reaction-formation*, he would call me a "lovely lady." Similarly he would kick my leg and then kiss it. I interpreted his behavior by telling him that he wanted to hurt me and then make the hurt go away. James exhibited his *identification with the aggressor* every time he unconsciously feared I might want to take his penis. At such times, beginning during the opening phase of the analysis, he imitated my feminine gestures and behavior in an exaggerated and hostile way. This was a repetition in the transference of his identification with his grandmother who aggressively put males down in a castrating way. Eventually, as I interpreted his defenses, he would laugh and say, "Only joking." He was developing an observing ego.

Working with their individual psychotherapists, James's parents realized that they had difficulty saying "No" to him. Gradually, they then became able to give him appropriate limits. He then quickly became more independent and learned to tie his shoes and tell time. Although he progressively became less feminine, and engaged in more masculine activities such as playing with boys, his intrapsychic fantasies and fears of castration remained unchanged. For example, he continued to interrupt his wedding games before they consummated in thoughts of female genitalia or sexual intercourse. After I pointed out these defensive interruptions many times, James began to play that Ken was putting his penis in Barbie's vagina. Barbie would then take Ken's penis, and Ken would be left with a vagina. James would scream "Ken lost his penis!" Often he said, "If you dress and act like a girl, nobody will think you have a penis. Then you don't have to worry that anyone will take it."

During the middle phase of the analysis, James's mounting hostile-aggressive transference-resistance developed into a full-blown transference neurosis. This was both disruptive to our sessions and unpleasant for me. He frequently requested that I put every one of Barbie's hairs into a bun. I always questioned why he wanted me to do this. Eventually, I told him that it was time for him to tell us why he wanted me to do this, or I would not do it anymore. Instead of explaining, he began to hit me with the Barbie doll. He was very anxious, and his escalating destructive behavior eventually forced me to interrupt many sessions. I asked him if he was trying to get me to say "No" to him because his parents seldom did. I worked on interpreting this resistance for several weeks. He finally stopped hitting me and began to put his transference wish to be told "No" into words, while simultaneously acting it out in play with the dolls. For example, instead of hitting me with Barbie, he began swinging her precariously on a circus trapeze while saying that she should have no hairs sticking-out because that would be "even more dangerous."

The next session, he expressed much anger at the director of a school "play" for *not* giving him a part. He had displaced onto the director of the "play" the anger he had toward me for stopping him from hitting me in "play therapy." Then, for the first time, he began to play ball with me. This masculine behavior strongly contrasted with the girls' games, such as with dolls, that he had played with me before. Next, he began to visualize penises in my office pictures. I told him that his anger about not getting a part in the school play seemed to have led him to see penises all over. He responded, "A penis is anger." He said that although he would like to know what it was like to be a woman, he would still like to be a man. In the past he had told me that I was "lucky" to be a woman; so I asked him whether his wish to be lucky like a woman had anything to do with his wish to keep all Barbie's hairs in a bun. James adamantly said, "No hair is to stick-out, not even one." I asked him if he worried about anything sticking-out from him. He said, "A penis." When I asked if having the hair all in place was like not having his penis stick-out, his play immediately reverted to the perilous trapeze act, and he threw Barbie around the room. He had her lose her shoes, which represented her penis and her power to him. James's behavior kept getting wilder and became dangerous to himself and to me. I said "No," he could not do that. James responded, "Do you want me to kill you?" I replied, "You think you're so powerful because you feel you can get away with anything with your grandmother and mother." He then settled down and again began to play ball with me. Why my saying "No" so greatly affected James, now became evident: He told me that it was bad to be a woman because women have four penises. "Two high-heels and two boobs make four penises. They can even have 25 penises," James said, "You can have press on nails, some on your toes, some on your hands, and a nose. It's bad because men can have only one penis." James explained that a penis is something that sticks-out, and that things that stick-out, like noses and hair, are penises. I asked him about my hidden penis that he used to talk about. He said it was the one stolen from Ken—the one women get back. I asked him, "*How* do they steal penises?" He replied, "They steal penises because they are jealous of men, and men's penises are real penises, but women just have ones that stick-out." "Men," James continued, "have one real one, and women want a real one, so they make things stick out[6]

---

[6]James had insight into the gesturing of hysterical women who seduce men with their body language and revealing, seductive clothing.

. . . Barbie needs a real one." I asked, "How is she going to get it?"
"Steal one," he replied. "Women come to the men at night and steal their
penises. They have pinchers. They use two of their penises. The press-on
nails are their pinchers. . . . But no woman will ever get mine." He added
that when you dress like a girl, these kinds of women won't know you
have a penis that they would like to have. Then James confided in me,
"I had one once. . . . I mean, I once had no penis." (He was referring to
the recent past when his parents and grandmother let him get away with
things. Once his parents began saying "No" to him, he could say "No" to
himself, which meant to him that he had a penis.) I asked, "When was
that?" He answered, "When men know how to say 'no,' they get their
penises back. Whenever men *don't* say 'no', women take their penises,
and when men say 'no,' they get them back. That's why only some men
don't have one." (Thus, because I had not said "No" to him, James thought
I lacked power. This meant to him that, like his grandmother, I lacked a
penis and, therefore, would want to steal his. So he hit me to test me and
see whether I would be impotent and helpless, or powerful and say "No"
to him. After I said "No" to him, he felt I had power. This meant to him
that I had a penis and no longer needed his. So he stopped hitting me.)
James went on to say that I didn't have those long fingernails like his
grandmother, and so how could I catch the ball. He said the ball was a
penis, and he wanted me to catch it. When it dropped, he said the penis
was gone. James asked to have my Great Dane at his next session.

In that session James continued to play with the ball, which he now
called a penis. He occasionally threw it to the Dane to see if the dog
would bite it. Afterward he said, "Nothing on ladies is supposed to stick
out. Because if it did, men would know they stole penises." He had
wanted me to wear a bun and not have any hair stick-out so that I would
not be like his envious grandmother who wanted to steal penises. I asked
him why I would do that. He replied that women steal penises because
they are jealous of men. I asked if anyone was jealous of him, and he said
that I was. He added that he didn't say "No" to his wish to do what he
was not supposed to do, because he didn't want me to be jealous of him.
If he said "No" to himself, it would mean he had a penis, which was his
power. He felt that then, like his grandmother, I would be jealous of his
penis (his power) and would want to steal it from him. If, like his grandmother, I had long nails and very high heels, that would mean I wanted a
real one, that is, a real penis, to stick-out. Thus, James saw me in the
transference as he had seen his grandmother. He saw me as putting him

down, and he felt I was envious of his penis. When I began to explicitly say "No," in words, to his aggressive, dangerous behavior, in his mind I gained power, that is, symbolically I gained a penis. This meant to him that I had my own strength and did not need his phallic power. He then felt safe and could verbalize why he had to not say "No" to himself and had to be aggressive toward me.

When, in her own psychotherapy, James's mother learned how her reaction-formation had prevented her from appropriately saying "No" to him, she began setting limits on him, and his fear of her diminished. He eventually realized that both with his mother and with me in the transference he was setting up situations to provoke us to say "No" to him. This had been a repetition compulsion.

During the first two years of the analysis James would crawl under my chair and look up to see if he could find my hidden penis. He often called me Dr. "Poop" (feces). He also said that my poop (my hidden penis) was powerful, and that if I would "poop" on him, I would make him into a girl. As we now continued to play ball, James recovered a significant early memory. He told me that, when he was about three, he had seen both a baby girl being diapered and his grandmother undressing. He saw their nude, genital areas. He said that he then had thought that girls were made backward and had their "poop holes" in front and their penises hidden in back. He had thought that they had lost their penises and had feared that this might happen to him. He had tried to *deny* castration *in fantasy* by imagining that women had penises that were, like feces, hidden in back. We now understood why in the middle phase of the analysis he had tried to slap my buttocks. It was to discover my "hidden penis." Thus, in the transference he felt more secure when he fantasied that he had given me a fecal penis. This helped maintain the therapeutic alliance. He said that he had dressed girl dolls in fancy clothing, like his grandmother's, to hide their "yucky" bottoms, which they had instead of penises.

During his analysis, in his play with female super heroes, he pretended he was a castrator rather than being castrated. He pretended he was Wonder Woman[7] restraining dolls with her powerful rope (that is, her penis) and locking them in boxes. Then he would release the dolls and have them fly away. Next, he would pretend he was Wonder Woman removing dolls' legs so they could not run away. Then he put their legs back. He said that

---

[7] The flying nun represented the phallic woman for Carlos like Wonder Woman did for James.

if Wonder Woman and the super-hero female characters had their own powers (that is, penises), they would not need to take the dolls' powers (that is, their penises) away from them. James's explained that he enjoyed playing with and imitating super-hero female characters like Wonder Woman because they had penises and were, therefore, powerful. Unlike his grandmother, they did not need to take penises from men. He also acted out this defense of identification with the aggressor in the transference by copying my feminine gestures whenever he feared that I might castrate him. He was fascinated, but frightened, when things came apart in my office. For example, when he accidentally pulled the tassel off my pillow, he asked me to sew it back. Then he pulled it off again and asked me to sew it back again. Working on this repetitious play enabled him to recognize that it symbolized his fear that he might lose his penis and become a girl.

We, thus, learned [from (1) his play with Wonder Woman and the dolls, (2) his identification with my dog and me, and (3) his fear of things coming apart] that he had defended himself against his fear of his aggressive, envious, and potentially castrating grandmother by identifying with her. By thus pretending to be a girl he concealed his penis and prevented his grandmother from envying it and trying to steal it. He also told me that he had thought that his grandmother had caused his grandfather's arm to shrivel.

When James was nine years old, after we had done much analytic work and he had greatly improved, his grandmother returned from a two-year absence, and he relapsed. He stopped saying "No" to his aggressive behavior, and his feminine speech and gestures returned. He noticed that these symptoms were worse around his grandmother. In his play with me he had a storm come and destroy the doll house. Then the doll furniture became too big to fit in the doll house. We learned that this play symbolized his fear that his penis might get big when he was near his grandmother. In the next session, while demonstrating his grandmother's seductive movements, he told me that the day before his grandmother had seductively encouraged him to feel her soft, black leather pants. He had become sexually aroused, had begun to get an erection, and had become anxious. He proudly told me that this time he had said, "No." He had refused to feel her soft pants. He remembered that when his grandmother had been seductive with him in the past, he had acted like a girl.

James's parents reported that he was again sleepwalking. He would walk to the toilet, flush it many times, and then go back to bed. During the day, when his grandmother was around, he also went to the bathroom frequently. In play with me, he had Ken and Barbie fight or run away from each other so that Barbie would not make Ken's penis feel "special" and want to take it away from him. We learned from this play that, when he got an erect penis around his grandmother, he became anxious because unconsciously he feared that she would envy it, want it, and take it. He then became consciously aware that he had been going to the bathroom frequently to reassure himself that he still had his penis. His frequent trips to the bathroom, his feminine behavior, and his sleep-walking then stopped.

Within and outside the analysis James gradually became more masculine. He stopped playing the role of a girl and began to enjoy climbing trees and bicycling with male friends. Boys began to invite him to their parties. At this point James's mother spoke to James and me and told us that she feared James "might get hurt" because he was getting so "vigorous" and active. Both James and I could see that she was trying to inhibit him and put him down. I suggested that she talk about her fears with her own therapist.

James worked-through in the transference and understood, that his wish to be a girl was an attempt to resolve his conflict between his biological masculinity and his fear of his grandmother's and mother's castrating behavior. He now rapidly progressed developmentally, and we were able to work-through and understand his triadic, oedipal relationships with his primary caregivers.

Follow-up of James at Age Fifteen

At age fifteen, James described himself as happy with a good sense of humor. He said he had the usual ups and downs. He prided himself for receiving a school award for being the friendliest student. With a smile he said that he had not been the nicest person when he was seeing me in analysis. Besides his high scholastic performance, he was active in extracurricular activities. He participated in drama and choir, and he competed in gymnastics and track. He remembered that when he was young he had not accepted himself as a boy and was jealous of girls because they were what he wanted to be. He did not know if he really wanted to be a girl or if he was just not happy with himself. His grandmother, he said, created the problem by influencing him to look at and wear her clothes and wear her shoes. She didn't say "No." He added that his mother didn't say "No" to him either. Laughingly, he said saying

"No" was no longer a problem for him. He said his "fancy grandmother" still looked like she was forty, and she still could say "No" to him or to his father. When she visited, he mostly went to his room, but he did spend some time with her because she was his grandmother.

James no longer had nightmares and had no memory of the nightmares he had as a child. He did not remember his play with Barbie. The only time he now felt anxious was when he acted in plays. He smiled when I asked if he had any homosexual feelings and told me that he had no interest in boys. His best friend was a boy. Half his friends were girls and half were guys. He did remember that after the analysis finished, his friends were mostly girls. For a few months after the analysis, he missed talking to someone, but he learned to deal with things himself. Now he enjoyed talking to his oldest brother and his friends.

Without my asking, he talked about people who—like one of his brothers—never learned to say "No" to themselves. They had trouble with teachers. James said he has learned to tolerate people's troubles. "No," he said, is a powerful word. James said he had no trouble saying "No" to friends when they offered him alcohol or drugs.

Getting close to girls was no problem. He didn't want a close relationship as yet, but went to dances and looked forward to having intercourse when the time was right. He asked me for information about female masturbation and had some hesitancy discussing his own masturbation. He concluded our talk by saying we brought back old moments and an awareness of the past. As he left, he said he would never hesitate to call me if he again became anxious.

James: Discussion

James's transsexual symptoms, like those of Carlos, were the result of an unconscious conflict. Before three-and-one-half James saw both his grandmother's and a baby girl's genitals and *denied in fantasy* (Freud, 1940) what he saw to reduce his fear of castration. Like Freud's Wolf Man, he fantasied that girls had their "poop holes" in front and their penises in back (Freud, 1918, p.25). Then, when his grandmother dressed him in girls' clothing, he concretely thought that she was preparing him for eventual castration and conversion into a girl. His grandfather's shriveled arm made this fantasied possibility seem real. Faced with a conflict between his biologically determined masculinity and his grandmother's hostile, envious, castrating behavior, James protected his penis from her by *identifying with* her as *the aggressor* and pretending he was a girl.

James repeated this process of *identification with the aggressor* in the transference, both with my feared dog and with me. He pretended to be a dog, and not a boy with a penis, so that the dog would not "bite off" his penis. He acted like a girl with me when in the transference he saw me as aggressive and abandoning, such as the time I told him we would have to stop our session if he did not stop trying to hurt me.[8] Thus, like Greenson's (1966), Loeb and Shane's (1982), McDevitt's (1985), and Arlow's (1987) patients, James attempted to master the traumatic threat of castration by identifying with the aggressor.

Although child analysts maintain that one should not play the parental role by saying "No" to child patients, I had to say "No" to James. The child analyst must not limit the child-patient's free-play, but must say "No" when the child's behavior becomes dangerous either to himself or the analyst. Dangerous behavior exceeds the bounds of free-play (the equivalent of free-association) and breaks the therapeutic contract.

I said "No" to James in the analysis for two different reasons. In the beginning of the analysis I had to say "No" to James and stop his sessions when his behavior went beyond play and became realistically dangerous and destructive. I told James he could hit my doll, but not me, and I told him that he could "fly" my doll, but not climb my furniture. This first limit established a boundary within which the therapeutic process could safely proceed. Later in the analysis, when James's repetitive play became a transference-resistance, I limited his play by asking him to put into words what he had been acting out in play. For example, I told him that I was no longer going to put Barbie's hair in a bun unless he told me why he wanted me to do so. This second "No" encouraged him to verbalize, and thereby make conscious, the unconscious meanings he was acting out in his play (Freud, 1915). When he resisted doing this by acting out destructively toward me, I had to apply the first limit again by telling him that either his destructive behavior would have to stop, or I would have to end the session. Eventually, we both learned that when I said "No" to him, it unconsciously meant to him that, unlike his grandmother and mother, I had my own power and did not need his penis.[9]

---

[8]There is also a history of actual abandonment and recurrent transference theme of abandonment in an adult male transsexual that I am now seeing in analysis.

[9]I had not seen Carlos long enough to interpret his wish to have me say "No" to him.

In James, what first appeared to be a prolonged symbiotic relationship with his mother turned out instead to be an identification with his aggressive grandmother. His transsexual wish was not the result of a fixation at the symbiotic phase of the separation-individuation process. Instead, it was the result of a defensive process that he found necessary for psychological survival.

Because James's father was distant, and both parents were passive, James's impulses could not be kept in check by his identification with either parent. Therefore, to establish adequate superego control he had identified with his aggressive, castrating grandmother. In the transference-neurosis, he unconsciously perceived my "No's" to mean that, unlike his grandmother, I had my own power (penis), and, therefore, I did not need to steal his power (penis). He also unconsciously construed my "No's" to be those reasonable limits that he had wished for, but had not received, from his parents. As we worked through his wish to have me say "No" to him, he became able to disregard his excessively limiting superego-identification with his grandmother. Then his internalized image of his weakly limiting father became more adequate. Carlos had also developed an excessively controlling superego by identifying with his castrating mother instead of with his absent and passive father.

GENERAL CONSIDERATIONS ABOUT TRANSSEXUALISM

Discussion of Carlos's and James's Analyses

A therapist need not be male to help transsexual patients. It is past object relationships, and not the sex of the analyst, that determines what is transferred onto the analyst. Developing a masculine identification with a surrogate father figure does have therapeutic value for transsexuals, but this approach is limited because it does not address or resolve transsexuals' underlying unconscious conflicts, which in my patients related to their mothers. I did not directly encourage either boy's masculine striving. Instead, I remained neutral by accepting their penises and their actual maleness. A therapist of either sex must be able to recognize both mother and father transferences, accept them, and help the patient work them through. Therapists' failures to recognize all transference manifestations in transsexual patients of any age, including preoedipal mother transference reactions, have led to the destructive acting out of such patients' unconscious conflicts, e.g., actual surgical castration.

Both of the transsexual boys that I analyzed had come into conflict with a maternal caretaker's negative attitude toward their boy's sexuality. Each boy dealt with this conflict by internalizing it and identifying with their maternal caretaker. This resulted in a gender identification reversal. Psychoanalysis allowed each boy to establish a realistic view of his gender identity.

Carlos saw his mother reject his father for being masculine. To avoid a similar rejection (abandonment), Carlos conflictually wished for castration. He wished he had no penis and imagined he was a girl. These symptoms intensified each time Carlos saw his mother drive his father out of the house. Thus, faced with a conflict between his biologically determined masculinity and his internalized representation of his mother's aversion to his masculinity, Carlos chose to renounce his masculinity so he could maintain his state of dependency on his mother.

Because James's grandmother envied men, she stimulated his masculine desires by seductively exhibiting her genitals to him, and then she hostilely thwarted his male proclivities by dressing him as a girl. This behavior made James fear that his envious grandmother might want to take his penis away from him, just like, as he fantasied, she had wasted his grandfather's arm. James defended against this possibility in two principal ways. First, he *denied in fantasy* (Freud, 1940) his observation that his grandmother lacked a penis by imagining that she had 25 penises. Second, he unconsciously *identified with his aggressive* grandmother (Freud, A., 1936/1966) by becoming effeminate. This concealed his penis so that she would not become envious and remove it. To master his traumatic experiences with his grandmother, he subsequently repeatedly acted out his unconscious identification with her by pretending to be a girl. When he acted out this feminine identification in his transference relationship with me, I was able to help him trace it back to his grandmother. Once he did this, he gave up his transsexual symptoms. Following his second analysis Carlos had also given up his identification with his aggressive, seductive mother.

In their analyses Carlos and James each learned that they did not have to give up either their masculine gender identity or their autonomy to enjoy the role of a child dependent on an adult. Before their analyses, neither Carlos's nor James's father could become the "bridge" that Roiphe and Galenson (1973) described as necessary for a boy to achieve individuation. This was fostered during the analyses when both fathers spent more time with their sons.

Carlos's and James's mothers each learned in their own psychoanalytic psychotherapy how they had pushed their sons toward femininity. Carlos's mother had not only sought to re-experience a closeness with her own mother through Carlos, she had also tried to prevent him from usurping her unconsciously held male position. Her hostile dependency and her bisexual conflict had clearly acted as a developmental interference (Nagera, 1966) for Carlos. James's mother and grandmother each frightened him with the possibility of the loss of his penis, which also acted as a developmental interference.

Both boys had been unconsciously aware of their female caregivers' dislike and envy of both their own and their fathers' masculinity. Each boy unconsciously reacted to this by wishing his penis was gone, by pretending it was not there, and by feeling and behaving like a girl. Faced with a conflict between their biologically determined masculine inclinations and their female caregivers' aversion to masculine behavior, they both chose to renounce their masculinity so that they would not be abandoned.[10] After both boys' transference feelings of rejection and abandonment had been worked through in some detail, both boys transferred their parents' phallic qualities onto me. Then, both became more phallic, masculine, and aggressive and began to talk about monsters that came at night. Carlos's monsters were nonspecific, while James had nightmares of lobsters pinching off penises. These monsters represented their projected anger and their castration fears. After their monsters were analyzed, the boys' hostile behavior toward me decreased.

The exaggerated, seductive, effeminate gesturing of my two young transsexual patients was a repetition-compulsion in which, in an effort to achieve mastery (Freud, 1920), they actively instead of passively repeated their original traumatic experiences of having been threatened with symbolic castration. If these boys had not gained insight through psychoanalysis, their repetition-compulsion to get revenge on a substitute (Freud, 1920 p.17) could, in the future, have provoked others to castrate them.

Pruett and Dahl's (1982) three patients, like my two patients, saw women's shoes as phallic symbols that represented power. Their patients also had other fantasies and symptoms, similar to those of my patients. For example: In Cinderella play, Bryan, age three-years-nine-months,

---

[10]Subsequently, when I analyzed an adult male transsexual, I learned that he longed for his mother not because he had had a blissful symbiotic relationship with her, but because she had ignored and abandoned him both psychologically and physically.

told other boys to put on a dress because it looked like armor. Buddy said that it felt so good and safe to be dressed as a girl. Bruce called himself "sister" in family drawings and, like my patient Carlos (Loeb and Shane, 1982) and Arlow's patient (1987), pulled his penis down between his legs and said "gone."

Greenson's (1966) and McDevitt's (1985) observations of boys with transsexual symptoms were similar to mine. Like my two patients, their patients had maternal caregivers that were both overly-gratifying orally and overly-seductive and frustrating genitally. Lance (Greenson, 1966) and Billy (McDevitt, 1985) looked up under their mother's and Barbie's skirts, while my two patients not only looked under Barbie's skirt, but also tried to look up under mine. Both of my patients made a spontaneous initial transference to me when they began the analyses by imitating my feminine walk and voice. They did this to conceal their penises so I, who they felt had none, would not be tempted to steal theirs. These imitations were identifications with me as a potential aggressor. Similarly, Lance (Greenson, 1966) did everything Greenson did, and Billy (McDevitt, 1985) put on McDevitt's hearing aid and glasses. Their patients, like mine, also had physically or psychologically absent fathers. Greenson's conclusion was different from mine, whereas McDevitt concluded that his patient's " ... feminine identification was determined primarily by his need to selectively identify with those traits of the maternal representation that provided him with the best compromise solution, the solution that provided libidinal and aggressive satisfaction and served defensive purposes."

In 1985 Stoller wrote of the Carlos case, "Of those who question ... [my] non-conflict theory only Loeb and Shane (1982) have presented observations I would consider to the point of my argument. Other colleagues simply make generalizations, quote authorities, or give anecdotes taken from adult, non-primary transsexuals—observations that to me simply confirm the hypothesis that such people do not suffer the constellation I described" (Loeb and Shane, 1982).

My cases, along with Brody's (1994), Person's (1974a), and McDevitt's (1985) cases, are important because they conclusively show that transsexual psychopathology can be the consequence of unconscious conflicts, which can be resolved through psychoanalytic treatment. These psychoanalytic findings are consistent with Socarides's (1970) view that the gender identity problem in transsexuals is due to intrapsychic conflict.

CONCLUSION

In both of my cases, transsexualism developed out of unconscious conflict. In both cases this symptom complex was the result of the boy being caught between *separation anxiety* and *castration anxiety*. The boys defended against this conflict mainly by *identifying with the aggressor.*[11] Thus, when a young boy's maternal caregiver exhibits her genitals to him, and simultaneously aggressively rejects his masculinity by treating him like a girl, he becomes anxious and may protect himself from feared castration and abandonment by unconsciously identifying with this envious, seductive, hostile woman. In so doing he pretends he is a girl to conceal and protect his penis and to assure continued nurturing. Thus, each boy felt that he could have either a penis or a maternal caregiver, not both. During their analyses, Carlos's and James's major conflict, their desire to, and dread of, pleasing their castrating female caregivers, was transferred onto me. We worked to clarify and understand this conflict, and their symptoms abated.

REFERENCES

ABELIN, E. (1977). *The Role of the Father in Personality Development.* Psychotherapy Tape Library. New York: Psychotherapy & Social Science Book Club.

ARLOW, J.A. (1987). Trauma, Play and Perversion. *Psychoanalytic Study of the Child.* 42:31–44.

COATES, S., FRIEDMAN, R.C., & WOLFE, S. (1991). The Etiology of Boyhood Gender Identity Disorder: A Model for Integrating Temperament, Development, and Psychodynamics. *Psychoanalytic Dialogues.* 1(4):481–523.

FREUD, A. (1936). The Ego and the Mechanisms of Defense in Volume II of *The Writings of Anna Freud.* New York: International Universities Press, pp. 109–121, 1966.

——— (1965). Normality and Pathology in Childhood: Assessments of Development in Volume VI of *The Writings of Anna Freud.* New York: Internatinoal Universities Press, pp. 36–43, 1966.

FREUD, S. (1905). Essays on the Three Theories of Sexuality. *Standard Edition* 7, 125–243.

---

[11] When each boy was caught between the danger of separation (his fear of the loss of the maternal object) and the danger of castration (his fear of the loss of his penis), he became anxious and defended himself by identifying with the aggressor (the aggressive woman) (Freud, A., 1936/1966).

———— (1908). The Sexual Theories of Children. *Standard Edition* 9:205–226.

———— (1910). Leonardo Da Vinci and a Memory of His Childhood. *Standard Edition* 11:59–138.

———— (1915). The Unconscious. *Standard Edition* 14:159–217.

———— (1918). From the History of an Infantile Neurosis. *Standard Edition* 17:3–124.

———— (1920). Beyond the Pleasure Principle. *Standard Edition* 18:3–64.

———— (1927). Fetishism. *Standard Edition* 21, 149–157.

———— (1940). An Outline of Psycho-analysis. *Standard Edition* 23: 141–207.

GELEERD, E.R. (1969). Separation-individuation: Introduction to Panel on Child Psychoanalysis. *International Journal of Psychoanalysis* 50:91–95.

GREEN, R., STOLLER, R.J. & NEWMAN, L.E. (1972). Treatment of boyhood transsexualism. *Archives of General Psychiatry* 26:213–217.

———— (1974). *Sexual Identity Conflict in Children and Adults*. New York: Basic Books.

———— (1976). One-hundred-ten Feminine and Masculine Boys: Behavioral Contrasts and Demographic Similarities. *Archives of Sexual Behavior*. 5(5):425–446.

———— (1987). *"The Sissy Boy Syndrome" and the Development of Homosexuality*. New Haven and London: Yale University Press.

GREENACRE, P. (1953). Penis Awe and its Relation to Penis Envy. In *Drives, Affects, Behavior*. ed. R.M. Loewenstein. New York: International. Universities Press, pp. 176–190.

GREENSON, R. (1966). A Transvestite Boy and a Hypothesis. *International Journal of Psychoanalysis* 47:396–403.

HARRISON, S. & CAIN, A. (1968). The Childhood of a Transsexual. *Archives of General Psychiatry* 19:28.37.

JACOBSON, E. (1964). *The Self and the Object World*. New York: International Universities Press.

LIMENTANI, A. (1979). The Significance of Transsexualism in Relation to Some Basic Psychoanalytic Concepts. *International Review of Psychoanalysis* 6:139–153.

LOEB, L., SHANE, M. (1982). The Resolution of a Transsexual Wish in a Five-year-old Boy. *Journal of the American Psychoanalytic Association* 30:419–434.

———— (1992). Analysis of the Transference Neurosis in a Child with Transsexual Symptoms. *Journal of the American Psychoanalytic Association* 40:587–605.

MAHLER, M., PINE, F. & BERGMAN, A. (1975). *The Psychological Birth of the Human Infant*. New York: Basic Books.

MCDEVITT, J.B., (1985). Pre-oedipal Determinants of an Infantile Gender

Disorder. Presented at the *International Symposium on Separation-Individuation*: "A Childhood Gender Identity Disorder: Analysis, Preoedipal Determinants, and Therapy in Adolescence," published in *The Psychoanalytic Study of the Child,* Vol. 50:79–105, 1995.

MEYER, J. (1974). Clinical Variants among Applicants for Sex Reassignment. *Archives of Sexual Behav*ior 3:527–668.

MEYER, J.K., & DUPLIN, CAROL, B.A. (1985). Gender Disturbance in Children. *Bulletin of the Menninger Clinic.* 49(3):236–269.

MEYER, J.K. (1982). The Theory of Gender Identity Disorders. *Journal of the American Psychoanalytic Association.* 30:381–418.

NAGERA, H. (1966). *Early Childhood Disturbances, the Infantile Neurosis, and the Adult Disturbances* New York: International Universities Press.

NEWMAN, L.E. & STOLLER, R.J. (1971). The Oedipal Situation in Male Transsexualism. *British Journal of Medical Psychology* 44:295–303.

PERSON, E. & OVESEY, L. (1974a). The Transsexual Syndrome in Males: I. Primary Transsexualism. *American Journal of Psychotherapy* 28:4–20.

———— (1974b). The Transsexual Syndrome in Males: II. Secondary Transsexualism. *American Journal of Psychotherapy* 28:174–193.

PRUETT, K.D., DAHL, E.K. (1982). Psychotherapy Of Gender Identity Conflict in Young Boys. *Journal of the American Academy of Child Psychiatry.* 21:65–70.

ROIPHE, J. & GALENSON, E. (1973). The Infantile Fetish. *Psychoanalytic Study of the Child.* 28:147–168.

SPERLING, M. (1963). Fetishism in Children. *Psychoanalytic Quarterly* 32:374–392.

———— (1968). The Analysis of a Boy with Transvestite Tendencies. *Psychoanalytic Study of the Child.* 19:470–493.

SOCARIDES, C.W. (1970). A Psychoanalytic Study of the Desire for Sexual Transformation ("Transsexualism"): The Plaster-of-paris Man. *International Journal of Psychoanalysis* 51:341–349.

STOLLER, R.J. (1967). Gender Identity and a Biological Force. *Psychoanalytic Forum.* 2(4):318–349.

———— (1968). *Sex and Gender: On the Development of Masculinity and Femininity* Vol. 1. New York: Taylor & Francis Group.

———— (1971). The term "transvestism." *Archives of General Psychiatry* 24:230–237.

———— (1973). The Male Transsexual as "Experiment." *International Journal of Psychoanalysis* 54:215–225.

———— (1975a). *Perversion.* New York: Pantheon Books.

———— (1975b). *Sex and Gender, Vol II. The Transsexual Experiment.* London: Hogarth Press.

———— (1985). *Presentations of Gender.* Yale University Press: New Haven and London.

TYSON, P. (1982). A Developmental Line of Gender Identity, Gender Role, and Choice of Love Object. *Journal of the American Psychoanalytic Association*. 30:61–86.

VOLKAN, V. & BERENT, S. (1976). Psychiatric Aspects of Surgical Treatment for Problems of Sexual Identification (transsexualism) in *Modern Perspectives in the Psychiatric Aspects of Surgery*, ed. J. Howells. New York: Brunner/Mazel. pp. 447–467.

WALINDER, J. & THUWE, I. (1975). A Social-psychiatric Follow-up Study of 24 Sex-reassigned Transsexuals. In *Reports from the Psychiatric Research Center*, ed. H. Forssman. Gotegorg, Sweden: Esselte Studium.

TRANSVESTITE SYMPTOMS IN AN ADOPTIVE FATHER AND GENDER-IDENTITY SYMPTOMS IN HIS ADOPTED SON DUE TO THE SAME EARLY ENVIRONMENTAL EXPERIENCES

Paul, who was described in Chapter 6, suffered from transvestitism. His adopted son, James, who was described in Chapter 7, suffered from a gender identity disorder. Because James was adopted, his sexual deviation could not have been genetically inherited from his adoptive father. Their separate, individual psychoanalyses revealed that their individual sexual deviations were caused, early in their childhoods, by Paul's mother's constant rejection of their masculine responses to her overly seductive sexual behavior. Her seductive and rejecting behavior led them each to develop an unconscious mental conflict between their masculine sexual drive and their fear of castration. Once, through their separate, individual psychoanalyses, they each became consciously aware of their respective conflicts, their sexually deviant symptoms diminished.

In this chapter we review and summarize the simultaneously seductive and rejecting behaviors of Paul's mother which led them each to develop their sexually deviant symptoms.

During His Psychoanalysis, Paul Discovered the Following Traumatic Experiences That Caused the Unconscious Conflicts That Manifested in His Transvestite Symptoms

During Paul's psychoanalysis, his repressed memories of his early experiences and fantasies emerged as anachronistic, disconnected, meaningless and unintegrated fragments. Through the psychoanalytic process, he gradually assembled these fragments into the following chronologically coherent, organized and meaningful, genetic-dynamic explanation of how and why both his distressing symptoms and maladaptive behaviors were formed. Once Paul achieved this conscious understanding, he was able to function more normally.

Until his fourth year Paul's mother undressed in front of him, slept with him, and changed her menstrual pads in front of him. She did not explain why she was bleeding, and he became both frightened and disgusted. In his fourth year Paul was taught—and believed—that his wishes would come true if he prayed to God. His belief in his magical-wish-power was reinforced when his mother praised him for taking apart a lawn mower, for making sparks fly by sticking a hair pin in an electric outlet, and for turning-off an escalator. When his father then returned home from the war, limping from a leg wound, Paul feared that the power of his wish to replace his father with his mother might have damaged his father's lower appendage.

Early in his fifth year, Paul watched his mother *remove* a little girl's diaper, and he saw that her penis was gone. He inferred that her penis had been *removed,* and he became terrified that his penis might also be *removed.* Several days later, he watched his mother *remove* a tight-fitting hand puppet from her hand. This reminded him that when his mother *removed* the little girl's diaper, she lacked a penis. He again became terrified that his penis might also be *removed.* Paul then repressed this terrifying thought by concealing it behind the following defensive rationalization: He *rationalized* that just as his mother's hand and fingers had been concealed behind the tight-fitting hand puppet, the little girl's penis must have been concealed behind a "tight-fitting girl-puppet suit." Thereafter, whenever he saw a puppet, robot, dummy, manikin, or doll that resembled a human, he would obsess about whether it was a real human or a counterfeit human. When he reached puberty, Paul began to obsess over whether an attractive woman was human or was a puppet, doll, robot, dummy, or manikin. Although he always knew that this obsessing was nonsensical and silly, he could not stop doing it until he learned, through his psychoanalysis, how and why it began.

Late in Paul's fifth year, while he was in a grocery store, he was carrying a balloon-on-a-stick in one hand while holding his penis in his other hand. He was playfully fantasying that his balloon-on-a-stick had magical power. He waved his balloon-on-a-stick toward a stack of Coca-Cola bottles wishing to magically topple them down without touching them with the balloon. Suddenly, without him or the balloon touching them, they all tumbled down. This experience reinforced his belief that he had magical-wish-power, and he became terrified. Soon after this, while batting a baseball toward his father, Paul had the wishful-thought that if he hit his father on the head with the baseball, his father would die, and that then Paul would again have his mother all to himself. He then feared that his wish-thought about the baseball, like his wish-thought about the balloon might have magic power and come true. Terrified, Paul dropped his bat and ran into the house crying. Paul then prayed, and asked—what he now, as an adult, called—"the powerful, Old Testament, punitive God of Retribution" to counteract Paul's malicious, magical-wish toward his passive, ineffectual, and crippled father. Unconsciously, Paul then retrospectively came to believe that his tonsillectomy at age three had been an anticipatory counter-magical punishment by the God of Retribution" for his subsequent wish to kill and supplant his father.

At age 13, because Paul's genital sexual drive was increasing, the intensity of his unconscious conflict between his genital sexual drive and his fear of castration also increased. At that time, he and his mother moved 200 miles away from his father, and shared a bedroom. While there, he twice became disgusted when he saw his mother's naked genital area. One day, as his mother got out of her car, her skirt rode up, and he saw her stockings, garter belt, and almost-see-through under panties. That evening, when alone, he put on her stockings, garter belt, and see-through under panties, looked at himself in a mirror, and masturbated to orgasm. This was the first time he cross-dressed and also the first time that he masturbated to orgasm. He said that this was his "most erotic experience." After ejaculating, he feared that the erotic thoughts that he had while masturbating might lead to his father's death. To protect his father—and to protect himself from potential retaliatory castration, Paul extended and elaborated the defensive rationalization that he had created when he was five. At five, when he saw a naked baby girl's genitalia, he had assumed that her penis had been cut off, and he had become afraid that his penis might also be cut off. To protect himself from his thought of castration, he had *rationalized* that the little girl's penis had not been cut off, but that it had been concealed behind a *skintight, girl-puppet suit*. At age 13, after seeing his mother's genitals hidden behind her almost-see-through under panties, he extended this defensive rationalization by *displacing* his sexual interest away from his mother's genital area and onto her *underclothing*—i.e., onto her *skintight girl-puppet suit*. These two defenses, *displacement* and rationalization, protected him both from his castration anxiety and from his unacceptable sexual attraction to his mother. After that, in order to ejaculate, he always had to look at himself in a mirror while wearing women's underwear—or fantasy that he was doing so. Because he closely resembled his mother, whenever he wore such underclothing and looked at himself in a mirror, he unconsciously saw his mother with a penis concealed beneath a *skintight girl-puppet suit*. Paul's transvestite cross-dressing—in addition to discharging his sexual drive—served four unconscious purposes: (1) It denied that women were castrated by demonstrating to him that their penises could be concealed beneath their underclothing. (2) It protected him from his terrifying thought that he might become castrated. (3) It concealed his repressed sexual desire for his mother. (4) It punished him for wanting to again supplant his father and be alone with his mother.

Near the end of his analysis Paul described these events in his fifth year as follows: "Both the balloon-on-a-stick and the baseball-bat events occurred at about the same time that I observed that the little girl lacked a penis. I linked these three events together with my tonsillectomy, my seeing my mother's menstruation, and my father's mutilated leg, and these experiences set the stage for all that happened within me after that."

During His Psychoanalysis, James Discovered the Following Traumatic Experiences That Led to the Unconscious Conflicts That Were Manifested in His Gender Identity Disorder

Between the ages of 1 and 4, James, unlike his heterosexual brother, spent a great deal of time in the care of his father's mother. She simultaneously aroused and thwarted James' masculine sexual impulses and was, therefore, psychologically castrating. During his psychoanalysis James explained that his grandmother always dressed in revealing, seductive clothing—which she often took off in front of him. He described her as a "nice lady" who "dressed fancy" to cover her "yucky body." She seldom said "No" to his requests, and, if he cried during the night, she would take him into her bed. Her permissiveness led him to believe that with her, he could "get away with anything." By the time he was 3, James had often seen his grandmother's naked genital area. He noticed that she lacked a penis and worried that he could lose his penis. His grandmother encouraged him to put on her clothing, jewelry, makeup, and high-heeled shoes. So he concluded that she wanted him to be a girl. This led him to fear that she was preparing him for eventual castration. This fear was reinforced by his belief that his grandmother might have injured his grandfather's leg.[1] To further defend against his fear that his grandmother wanted to take his penis, he attempted to please her by "unconsciously

---

[1] For purposes of confidentiality L. Loeb had called it an arm in Chapter 7.

identifying with her as an aggressor" (Freud, A., 1936)· Consequently, James both behaved effeminately and claimed that he was a girl in a boy's body. By telling people that he was a girl in a boy's body he was also concealing the fact that he had a penis so that his grandmother would not envy it and want to take it for herself.

The preceding unconscious psychodynamics were revealed as follows during James' psychoanalysis, which began when he was four-and-two-thirds years old. In play therapy, he dressed a Barbie doll in "plain" clothing, and called her "mother." He dressed another Barbie doll in "fancy" high heels and a low cut, strapless gown, and he called her "queen-grandmother." He demonstrated several times how queen-grand-mother's gown could slip down and expose her breasts. He said that he wished that the gown had straps. Eventually, he asked me [his analyst] to take off my clothes. This was an acting-out of his grandmother transference neurosis. He said that if I [his analyst]—like his grandmother—had long nails that stuck-out, and very high heels, that would mean I—like his grandmother—wanted a *real* penis to stick-out. From the beginning of his psychoanalysis, James broke my toys, spit at me, put his "snot" on me, lifted my skirt, and hit me. When I asked him why he wanted to hurt me, he replied that *he* did not want to hurt me, but that the monster that appeared in his nightmares did want to hurt me. In one such nightmare, he said that, *a half lady, half pinching-lobster-monster ran out of his mother's nose and was chasing him.* Excitedly he said, "lobsters can pinch." Such castration themes predominated in James' play. For example, he pretended to be Dorothy in the *Wizard of Oz*, who was seeking *red shoes* for herself, a *heart* for the Tin Man, a *brain* for the Straw Man, and *courage* for the Cowardly Lion. These absent parts all represented lost penises to him.

James frequently transferred his image of his grandmother onto me. He would feel that I was putting him down and feared that I wanted to take his penis. He then behaved like a girl and imitated my feminine voice and gestures. With me, James defended himself from his fear of castration by fantasying that I had 25 penises. This was a "denial in fantasy" of castration. Eventually, I helped him understand that he was transferring his aggressively seductive, rejecting, and castrating grandmother onto me and that he was then identifying with me as an aggressor as he had originally done with his grandmother. He learned that this identification had allowed him to retain—in a childlike way—both his grandmother's approval and his penis. Once he understood this, he became less afraid of losing his penis, and he was able to be more masculinely-aggressive toward me. Eventually, this aggressive, masculine behavior escalated to the point that it became hazardous, and I had to tell him to stop. When I told him to stop, he told me that—unlike his permissive grandmother—I had my own power, so I did not need to take his power, that is, his penis.

After I had set this limit, by saying no to his hazardous aggression, he felt safe enough to act out why he had become so aggressive toward me in his play. He played with Super-Women dolls and said that—unlike his grandmother—they had their own powers [i.e., penises], and so they did not need to take powers [penises] away from men. James then understood that he had believed himself to be a girl in a boy's body to defend himself against his grandmother's negative, castrating attitude toward his aggressive, masculine impulses. By believing himself to be a woman he had concealed his penis and prevented his grandmother from envying it and trying to "steal" it. Once James became consciously aware of all this, he was able to establish a realistic view of his male identity and accept himself as a boy. His gender-identity symptoms then diminished until, finally, they were no longer present.

When James was 9, his grandmother returned after a two-year absence, and he relapsed. His effeminate speech and gestures returned, and, once again, he became aggressive toward me. He said that his effeminate behavior was most exaggerated when he was around his grandmother. In his play, he had a storm destroy the doll house. Then he had the doll furniture become "too big" to fit in the doll house. A psychoanalysis of this play, allowed James to become consciously aware that he feared that his penis might become "too big" when he was near his grandmother. While imitating his grandmother's seductive movements, he told me that his grandmother had seductively encouraged him to feel her, tight, soft, black leather pants. When she did this, he had begun to get an erection and feared that she might become envious of his penis and wish to take it. Proudly, he told me that he had refused to feel her pants. He reaffirmed that he had behaved like a girl whenever his grandmother had behaved seductively toward him. This incident strengthened his conscious understanding of how he had identified with his aggressive grandmother, and his effeminate behavior again ceased.

I followed up James once, when he was 15, to see how he was doing. He was very masculine in appearance, exhibited no effeminate behavior, and had no identification as a female. I saw no need for James to have further psychoanalysis.

DISCUSSION

If James had been Paul's biological son, one could readily have assumed that James' transsexual, gender-identity symptoms were genetically inherited from his transvestite father. However, since James was adopted, this was not possible. Their separate psychoanalyses revealed that their similar sexual deviations were caused by Paul's mother's seductive, rejecting, and castrating behavior.

REFERENCE

FREUD, A. (1936). The Ego and the Mechanisms of Defense in *The Writings of Anna Freud* (Vol. II). New York: International Universities Press, 1966.

CONCLUSION

In this book we have presented summaries of a several psycho-analytic therapeutic processes of both adults and children who were suffering from various sexual deviations. None sought help because of their sexually deviate behaviors. As we worked with them on their current thought processes and their transference responses to us, we were able to help each of them become aware of, understand, and resolve their underlying unconscious sexual conflicts. During each treatment, we carefully avoided being influenced and biased by the psychiatric or psychoanalytic literature. Instead, we investigated psychoanalytically each of our patient's unconscious minds to discover and help them understand their individual and distinct psychodynamics. Through this approach, we corroborated many of Freud's and his followers' findings, and we discovered new facets of our patients' respective illnesses.

Following their treatment, all our patients were able to lead fulfilling heterosexual lives. The homosexual man described in Chapter 3 has become fully consciously aware of how and why he both feared women and could not allow himself to get sexually aroused with them. He is still working on establishing an affectionate and sexual relationship with a woman. After treatment, the two children who had gender identity problems could accept, and identify with, their biological gender. The maternal caretakers of all of our patients were overly seductive with them and overly rejecting of their masculinity.

In Chapters 5 and 6, we presented the successful treatment of two patients who suffered from transvestite symptoms. Both of their mothers had been exhibitionistic with them and both had seen their mother's menstrual pads. Oedipal conflicts were paramount in these two cases. Neither has worn women's clothing since their psychoanalyses.

In Chapter 7 we presented the psychoanalyses of two children who had gender identity problems. One child's mother and one child's grandmother had been exhibitionistic. Each child had a pathological unconscious conflict, which was resolved through the psychoanalysis of their transference neuroses.

Although, currently, some believe that people's sexual orientation is inevitably determined by genetics, we have shown that childhood experiences can lead to unconscious conflicts that manifest in sexual deviations. For example, in Chapters 6 and 7 we have presented two non-genetically related patients who developed similar sexual disturbances from the nearly identical environmental determinants. These two patients are jointly discussed in Chapter 8.

All of our patients were males. Each had either conscious and/or unconscious castration anxiety, and each had failed to resolve an unconscious conflict between his wish to be masculinely aggressive and his wish to attain his mother's approval. Unconsciously, they each felt that they had to give up either their masculinity [their penises] or their maternal figures. Thus, they were all trapped between their castration anxiety and their separation anxiety.

Our patients' treatments took place during the past 35 years. We followed them all up after varying periods of time and found that none of them lost the insight they achieved, nor the behavioral changes they acquired, through psychoanalysis.

INDEX

P

U

underclothes. *See* clothing/underclothes

unworthiness, feeling of, 79–80, 91–92, 98, 109

V

Volkan, V., 130

W

Walinder, J., 130

Wiedeman, George H., 7–9

The Wizard of Oz, 39, 54n3, 142, 163

women. *See also* penis, female; penis, female lack of

attitudes toward men, 95, 99, 104, 132–133, 152–153

in case study of Bill, 63–65

in case study of Cal, 12–13, 17–18, 20

in case study of Carlos, 132–133, 137

in case study of James, 146–147

in case study of John, 80, 86–88, 95, 98–100, 104–105

in case study of Paul, 110n1, 113

in case study of Pete, 26–29, 32–36, 38–39, 44–45, 60

castration of, 99–100, 105

compared to mother, 33–34, 36, 60, 87

fear of, 35

fear of dependence on, 45, 86

fear of sex with, 32, 36, 38–39

hostility to, 88, 95

phallic, 6–7, 137, 146–147

relationships with, 26–28, 34, 38, 44, 63–65, 80

transvestites as, 6–7

ABOUT THE AUTHORS

LORETTA R. LOEB, MD
(1932–2012)
Clinical Professor, Department of Psychiatry,
Oregon Health Sciences University

and

FELIX F. LOEB, JR., MD
Clinical Professor, Department of Psychiatry,
Oregon Health Sciences University

Distributed by Jason Aronson, Inc.

www.ingramcontent.com/pod-product-compliance
Lightning Source LLC
Chambersburg PA
CBHW072130020426
42334CB00018B/1736